insight text guide

Anica Boulanger-Mashberg

The Thing Around Your Neck

Chimamanda Ngozi Adichie

First published in 2014, reprinted in 2014, 2015 (twice), 2017 (twice), 2018, 2019, 2020, 2021, 2022, 2023.

Insight Publications Pty Ltd
3/350 Charman Road
Cheltenham VIC 3192
Australia
Tel: +61 3 8571 4950
Fax: +61 3 8571 0257
Email: books@insightpublications.com.au

www.insightpublications.com.au

National Library of Australia Cataloguing-in-Publication entry:
Boulanger-Mashberg, Anica, author.
Chimamanda Ngozi Adichie's The thing around your neck / Anica Boulanger-Mashberg.
9781922243676 (paperback)
Insight text guide.
Includes bibliographical references.
For secondary school age.
Adichie, Chimamanda Ngozi, 1977- The thing around your neck.
Adichie, Chimamanda Ngozi, 1977- —Criticism and interpretation.
823.92

Other ISBNs:
9781925175257 (digital)
9781925175585 (bundle: print + digital)

Cover design: The Modern Art Production Group

Printed by Markono Print Media Pte Ltd

contents

CHARACTER TABLE

Title	Central characters	Central themes and ideas
'Cell One'	Nnamabia; his unnamed sister	Violence; siblings/family; religion; agency
'Imitation'	Nkem; Obiora; Amaechi	Diaspora/immigrant experience; agency; marriage/fidelity
'A Private Experience'	Chika; unnamed Hausa woman	Religion; violence and conflict; identity; cultural difference
'Ghosts'	James; Ikenna	Nostalgia; national identity; violence and war
'On Monday of Last Week'	Kamara; Neil; Josh; Tracy; Tobechi	Agency; identity; marriage and fidelity; parenting
'Jumping Monkey Hill'	Ujunwa; Edward; Chioma	African identity; the nature of fiction
'The Thing Around Your Neck'	Akunna; her unnamed American boyfriend	Agency; identity; cultural difference
'The American Embassy'	Unnamed woman; her son Ugonna	Violence; diaspora/ immigrant experience; agency
'The Shivering'	Ukamaka; Chinedu	Diaspora/immigrant experience; male–female relationships; agency
'The Arrangers of Marriage'	Chinaza (Agatha); Ofodile (Dave)	Agency; identity; marriage; cultural difference
'Tomorrow Is Too Far'	Unnamed woman; Dozie; Nonso	Agency; family; gender; regret
'The Headstrong Historian'	Nwamgba; Obierika; Anikwenwa (Michael); Afamefuna (Grace)	Agency; religion; identity

OVERVIEW

About the author

Chimamanda Ngozi Adichie is an award-winning Nigerian writer born in 1977. She grew up in Nsukka, in south-eastern Nigeria, where a number of the stories in *The Thing Around Your Neck* (2009) are set. As a young woman she moved to America to study – including postgraduate studies in creative writing – and she now lives in both Nigeria and America. Much of her writing is concerned with experiences of being Nigerian.

Her first novel, *Purple Hibiscus*, set in Nigeria during a military coup, was published in 2003 and won a number of prizes, including the 2005 Commonwealth Writers' Prize for Best First Book. Her second novel, *Half of a Yellow Sun*, was published in 2006 and also won awards, including the 2007 Orange Broadband Prize for Fiction. It is set during the Nigerian–Biafran war for independence, and was inspired by her grandfathers, who both died as a result of the war. *Purple Hibiscus* and *Half of a Yellow Sun* have been made into films. Adichie's third novel, *Americanah* (2013), continues to explore themes of Nigerian identity and a Nigerian diaspora (particularly in America).

In addition to these novels, Adichie has published short stories in many literary journals, and some of these are republished in *The Thing Around Your Neck*. This collection includes stories of Nigerians living in Africa, and also tales of Nigerian immigrants in America. It has been shortlisted for a number of awards, including the 2010 Commonwealth Writers' Prize for Best Book (Africa).

While Adichie's stories are fiction, it is not uncommon for characters to share biographical details with their creator – for example, names, locations and situations. In an article in *The Guardian*, Adichie discusses the difference between memoir and fiction, writing, 'even when I base a character on a "real" person, the character is never quite that real person' (Adichie 2013). This is a reminder that while Adichie may be inspired by actual events and people, what we read in her short stories is still fiction.

Adichie's other published writing includes poetry, a play, and many essays and articles for journals and newspapers such as *The New York Times* and *The Washington Post*. She also teaches creative-writing workshops in Nigeria.

Synopsis

The Thing Around Your Neck comprises twelve short stories about Nigerian characters either in Africa or in America. The stories explore what it means to be Nigerian, whether as an immigrant or in Nigeria. Many of the central characters are young married women, but there are also older men, single women, young boys and a handful of non-Nigerian American friends, boyfriends, employers or neighbours. The notion of a Nigerian identity is central to the collection, though not necessarily foregrounded in every story.

The stories are independent of one another, although they often share settings, such as Nigeria in the 1990s during General Abacha's military regime. The stories may be read with little knowledge of postcolonial Nigerian history, but contextual understanding helps to deepen the meaning.

The stories address a range of themes and ideas, from the domestic to the political, which recur throughout the collection. These include:

- marriage, relationships and infidelity
- civil war and its long- and short-term impacts
- gender and power dynamics
- postcolonial identity
- family relationships
- wealth and poverty
- regret and lost opportunities
- immigrant experience and negotiating multiple cultures
- agency and fate.

Other themes covered include sibling relationships, religion and its role in conflict, representations of Africa, fiction as therapy, parenting and academic life.

While many of the stories are intimate in scope – featuring the individual, subjective experience of one or two characters, often during a short period of time – there are many ways in which Adichie encourages us to extrapolate from individual narratives to read a broader commentary on Nigerian identity. Some such techniques include:

- the shifting chronological perspective (for example, in 'A Private Experience')
- unnamed characters (for example, representatives of African nations in 'Jumping Monkey Hill')
- the use of the second-person perspective.

These techniques are discussed in more detail in later sections of this guide.

BACKGROUND & CONTEXT

Nigerian literary context

Adichie is one of a number of African writers who have been published to acclaim outside Africa. Her work, like that of many of her peers, tends to explore the experience of being African (specifically Nigerian). Nigerian writers who have preceded Adichie include Wole Soyinka, who won the Nobel Prize for Literature in 1986, and Chinua Achebe, who died in 2013 and was one of Africa's most celebrated authors. His 1958 novel, *Things Fall Apart*, explores the influence of British colonisation on Igbo culture and people. Adichie has acknowledged the influence of Achebe's work on her own and on that of other African writers. Like Achebe, Adichie's heritage is Igbo, but the work of both novelists is in English (Nigeria's official language) rather than Igbo.

Interestingly, Adichie grew up in the same house Achebe once lived in, although she did not realise the significance of this coincidence – growing up in the house once occupied by the writer whose work had been most influential on her – until well after she had begun her career as a writer.

Geography and history

All the settings in *The Thing Around Your Neck* are real places. Approximately half of the stories are set in various parts of America, and the other half in African countries. In the African stories, the location is important, though it is not always made explicit. Most are set in Nigeria (with the exception of 'Jumping Monkey Hill', set near Cape Town in South Africa), and specific Nigerian locations include the cities of Kano, Lagos and Nsukka.

Nigeria

The Federal Republic of Nigeria is a large country in the west of Africa, covering more than four times the area of Victoria, with an estimated population of more than seven times that of Australia, and a high rate of population growth. The country was federated after British colonisation in the late 1800s and remained part of the British Empire until 1960, when it became independent.

Kano

A large city in the north of Nigeria, Kano is heavily populated, and primarily Hausa Muslim. Hausa is one of the main languages. Kano is the capital of Kano State, and the groundnuts sold by the Hausa woman's daughter in 'A Private Experience' are one of the main commercial products of the state.

Nsukka

Nsukka is a small city in Enugu State in southern Nigeria. Principally an Igbo-speaking area, Nsukka is home to the University of Nigeria, where Adichie's father was a professor and where several of the characters in this collection have also worked (for example, the father in 'Cell One'; James Nwoye and Ikenna in 'Ghosts'). Nsukka was one of the towns in Biafra, and one of the first sites of conflict during the war, when Nigerian forces took the town and burnt the university (an event alluded to in 'Ghosts').

Lagos

Lagos is located in the south of Nigeria, in Lagos State, on the coastal edge of the country where the Gulf of Guinea meets the continent. It is the largest Nigerian city by population and one of the largest African cities. For most of the twentieth century, Lagos was the nation's capital, and though this is no longer the case, it remains an important trade port and commercial centre for the country.

'Which Africa?'

Adichie has expressed surprise and frustration that as a student in America, she was expected to represent not just Nigeria but also all of Africa. She has discussed differences between African nations, including in the article 'Our "Africa" Lenses' (Adichie 2006), and sometimes in her fiction (for example, in 'Jumping Monkey Hill'), emphasising the inaccuracy of referring to a singular African identity. While some experiences in this text represent an 'African' experience, most are more specific, representing Nigeria, Lagos or even a smaller milieu and culture (such as the university community in Nsukka).

Politics

British administration of the many geographical, religious and ethnic parts of Nigeria created an artificial sense of nationalism and homogeneity. The borders of the federated country did not take into account existing borders between ethnic and religious communities, and conflict between many of these groups continued after Nigeria attained independence from the British Empire in 1960.

As well as being made up of many different states, Nigeria is also populated by hundreds of different ethnic groups. The three largest – Hausa–Fulani, Yoruba and Igbo – make up the majority of the Nigerian population, and are often mentioned in the stories in *The Thing Around Your Neck*. Many of the central characters are of Igbo ethnicity, like Adichie.

The major religions in Nigeria are Christianity and Islam; religious divisions roughly align with geographical divisions, with more Christians in the south and Muslims in the north of the country. Minor religions include those of traditional cultures such as the Igbo. Most Igbo people, however, are Christian (though their Christianity is sometimes blended with Igbo beliefs and traditions), and most Hausa are Muslim. Historically, political divisions have also echoed geographical boundaries, with the largely Christian south accepting more of the British rule and influence, culturally and economically, than the north.

Nigeria has a history of internal conflict, and the Nigerian Civil War, or Nigerian–Biafran War (1967–70), was a significant event in the country's contemporary history. It occurred when many southern provinces attempted to gain independence from the colonially federated Nigeria by forming an alliance, the Republic of Biafra. Biafra existed for only three years, after its constituent provinces withdrew from federal administration. Existing tensions between territories and ethnic groups, and several military coups – resulting in numerous fatalities – precipitated the war, and during the fighting many civilian lives were lost, either to direct violence or in consequence of the conflict, including through starvation. Ultimately, the Republic of Biafra was poorly equipped against the well-resourced Nigerian federal forces, which also had support from the British, and in 1970 the Biafrans surrendered and the provinces were reabsorbed into the nation of Nigeria.

Many of Adichie's stories in this collection (as well as her other works) are set in the postwar period, or contain flashbacks to and reminiscences of events during the war, such as the fall of Nsukka. This occurred within weeks of the war's beginning, and forms the setting for significant sections of 'Ghosts'.

Chronology

Although the timeframes of the stories are often not clearly stated and dates are rarely given, chronology can often be deduced from the historical events mentioned. For example, the death of the First Lady in 'The Shivering' echoes the death of real-life First Lady Stella Obasanjo in 2005 (she died under the same circumstances as the First Lady in the story). While the story collection is a work of fiction and not a historical document, Adichie appears to present accurate timeframes that reflect actual history in Nigeria. Another example is the protests for democracy in 'A Private Experience', which situate the story somewhere during General Abacha's military regime (1993–98).

Q Do you think Adichie's fiction would have had the same success outside Africa if she had not written in English? Why or why not?

Q Adichie finds it unrealistic to characterise Africa as having a single, homogeneous culture. How realistic is it to identify and discuss a single national culture for a large country such as the United States (as Adichie does in many of these stories)?

GENRE, STRUCTURE & LANGUAGE

Short stories

A collection of short fiction allows for the telling of many stories that offer differing perspectives without the confusion that might occur if so many settings and characters were woven into a single narrative.

The short story is a form with fairly loose boundaries; for example, there are no firm rules about word limits. A short story must be shorter in length than a novel or novella, but it is not the shortest form of fiction. In contemporary Australian publishing, fictional works of fewer than 1000 words might be called micro-stories or flash fiction; works between 1000 and 19,000 words are described as short stories; works between about 20,000 and 50,000 words are categorised as novellas; and works of more than 50,000 words are regarded as novels.

However, such definitions can vary greatly, and are not always formal. For example, H. G. Wells, who often made use of the form, is said to have defined short stories as fiction that could be read in a quarter of an hour. Rather than relying on length, then, perhaps a simpler way to classify the short story is that it is unlikely to be published on its own, but rather found in collections (such as *The Thing Around Your Neck*) or in literary journals (where a number of Adichie's stories were first published).

A short story is a subgenre of fiction. Short non-fiction works are classified by other titles, such as articles or essays.

Postcolonial literature

Postcolonial theory is harnessed in many academic disciplines. In literary studies, it refers to a particular critical discourse (set of conventions, terms and theoretical ideas used to analyse and discuss works) that allows scholars to group literatures from various countries where European colonisation has influenced identity and traditional ways of life.

While these works are likely to differ greatly in content and style, postcolonial theory argues that there are themes and ideas common to the literature emerging from colonised nations. For example, the immigrant experience examined in *The Thing Around Your Neck* could be seen as representative of a nation that has experienced the outside influence of a colonial culture.

As an area of literary theory, postcolonialism is fraught with complex and ongoing academic debate, including about such seemingly minor details as whether to hyphenate the word (post-colonial or postcolonial); the hyphen is seen by some as imposing an artificial chronological marker for the beginning of a particular theoretical period.

The term 'postcolonial' in this guide is used much more simply, to refer to a time following a period of colonialism – here, after European colonisation of Nigeria – and to the kinds of thought and literature that might emerge from such a national cultural and political experience. Postcolonial writing such as Adichie's text belongs to a body of work that is of interest not only for its literary value, but also for where it sits in a social, political and philosophical landscape, and how it represents the experiences of a colonised nation.

Structure

The collection comprises twelve independent short stories. They are not interlinked by recurring characters, but many share chronological or geographical settings. Recurring themes also offer the collection a sense of cohesion. The stories do not necessitate reading in a particular order. But, just like words in a sentence or paragraphs within a narrative, the order of the stories has been chosen carefully, to maximise the impact of each and the shape of the collection as a whole.

The stories generally alternate between American and African settings, heightening the social, economic, geographical and political contrasts between the countries. This alternation between settings also helps Adichie to maintain readers' interest.

Narrative point of view

In three of the stories, the narrative is told from the central character's perspective, the **first-person singular** ('I'). Seven stories use the **third-person limited** perspective (referring to the central character using either the character's name or 'she' – all the third-person central characters in such stories are female), although sometimes exhibiting omniscience with regard to the narrator's knowledge of events. The third-person limited is a perspective closely tied to a particular character, as opposed to **third-person omniscient**, where the narrator has access to all possible information in the story, including the thoughts of multiple characters.

The remaining two stories employ a **second-person perspective** ('you'). This is a very unusual narrative perspective in fiction. It can be difficult to sustain without the writing becoming confusing or grammatically awkward. It can create a powerful connection between the reader and the material, and may be quite confronting. This is because it is hard for a reader to disengage while the writer is addressing them directly, and also because in non-fiction, the second-person voice is usually reserved for instructional writing, so readers can feel as though they are being lectured.

The differing perspectives are associated with the following impacts:

- first person – aligns readers with the central character, encouraging empathy with their situations and decisions
- second person – puts readers in the character's position, even more forcefully than the first-person perspective
- third person (limited) – can distance readers and foreground the writer's opinions or role; can also encourage connection with a particular character.

Language

Tense

In two stories, 'A Private Experience' and 'The Headstrong Historian', Adichie alternates between present and future tense. This unusual technique allows her to maintain continuity, while efficiently expanding the narrative beyond the scope otherwise available in short stories. For example, 'A Private Experience' is set during a single incident, but the narrator offers us a series of 'flash-forwards' into Chika's future, illustrating the significance and impact of present events. Here, the third-person perspective – while limited in terms of character – leans towards omniscience regarding timeframe, since the narrator conveys information Chika could not possibly know at the time.

Vocabulary

The Thing Around Your Neck is written in English, but many Igbo words make their way into the text. Often they are explained immediately; for example, 'all he said was "*Ndo,*" nothing more than "Sorry"' (p.64). In other cases, the context allows non-Igbo-speaking readers to deduce the likely meaning. For example, when Chinaza says '*Ike agwum*' (p.168), her new husband replies that he is exhausted too, suggesting that she has said something like 'I'm tired'.

There are a number of online vocabulary lists and translation engines for Igbo to English (one is listed in the 'References & Reading' section), but these resources should be used with caution. They are not exhaustive, and may not always give exact or accurate meanings.

In most stories the use of Igbo words is minimal, but in several the issue of language is raised by characters themselves. Examples include the following:

- In 'Cell One', Nnamabia, when apologising for stealing from his parents, speaks dramatically in 'English, using unnecessary words' (p.4).

- In 'Ghosts', James, when telling Ikenna about the deaths of his daughter Zik and wife, Ebere, deliberately chooses to speak in Igbo instead of English (p.64 and p.66).
- In 'The Arrangers of Marriage', Chinaza, after arriving in America, is ordered by her husband, Ofodile, to '[s]peak English' (p.177) rather than their traditional language.
- Ofodile also judges a woman and her two children who are speaking Spanish in the supermarket, arguing that they will never be able to integrate into American society if they insist on maintaining other cultural connections (p.175).

Many characters speak multiple languages, which is representative both of life in a colonised country and of life as an immigrant. Embracing a second language is symbolic of embracing a second culture, and many of Adichie's characters illustrate this with their choice of words.

Realism and symbolism

The text is primarily realist in style, describing concrete events and situations. Even the titles of the stories, such as 'The American Embassy', often refer directly to their content, rather than employing metaphor or symbolism. A notable exception is the title story, where the meaning remains subjective and ambiguous even after reading the story. The literal titles, however, can still imply multiple layers of meaning. For example, while 'Imitation' refers directly to the artworks in the story, it might also allude to the 'plastic' (p.24) culture of America – an imitation of a more visceral life in Nigeria. Or perhaps it describes the facade of a happy marriage.

Similarly, while the language throughout is often concrete and literal, Adichie does still use symbolism. An example is when Nkem showers with her husband and 'soaps his back' (p.41). The symbolism of the action demonstrates that she is serving him, as a 'good wife' should. Yet she is simultaneously steering their lives for the first time, telling him that she and the children are to move back to Nigeria with him. The symbolism creates a juxtaposition between action and speech.

STORY-BY-STORY ANALYSIS

Cell One (pp.3–21)

Summary: *Seventeen-year-old Nnamabia robs his family home; after a campus shooting, he is arrested; his family visit him in prison almost every day; he is transferred to Cell One for 'misbehaving' but is eventually released.*

'Cell One' tells the story of a young, headstrong, popular student who may or may not be involved with the increasingly violent university campus 'cults' (extreme, gang-like fraternity clubs). He is adored by his mother – who forgave him all manner of things as he grew up (pp.6–7) – and reluctantly admired by his sister, with a 'tenderness' that she 'could not have explained' (p.16). The first impression we are given of Nnamabia is that he is the kind of boy who will steal from his family because that is what the popular boys do. The last impression we are given is of him sacrificing his safety to stand up against unfair treatment of a fellow prisoner. In between, he is neither good nor evil, but both commits crimes and renounces cruelty. Like many of Adichie's characters, he is painted in shades of grey rather than in black and white.

This first story is our introduction to some of the text's themes and settings. Specific incidents or details in 'Cell One' represent broader ideas explored throughout the collection, for example:

- the unnamed narrator's conflicted relationship with her brother Nnamabia (challenges inherent in male/female relationships of various kinds – including between siblings – recur in many stories)
- the violence and corruption exhibited by prison officials (this echoes the social and political violence we see elsewhere)
- the prominence of religion; in the first paragraph, the central characters are seen habitually attending Mass.

Another important theme introduced in this story is the notion of *agency*: a character's level of control in his or her life. In 'Cell One', as in many other stories, events unfold with little sense that the central character is in control of their fate. Nnamabia, while possibly involved in one of the 'cults', has not necessarily played an active role in the violence on campus; he is arrested the next evening in a bar, having broken the nine o'clock curfew (p.9). Although we cannot be certain of his guilt or innocence, it seems probable that he is a pawn in some arbitrary game. This is reflected later when, after standing up for a fellow prisoner, he is punished with a transfer to the infamous Cell One (which has the worst reputation in the already overcrowded, violent jail). Shortly after, however, Nnamabia is released when a cult member turns informant, asserting that Nnamabia was not part of the cult. As with his arrest, Nnamabia's release seems connected to the actions of others, rather than to his own.

On the other hand, it could be argued that Nnamabia earns his freedom by risking his personal safety to stand up for a stranger: the old man being imprisoned unfairly and abused. His arrest could be seen as a symbolic punishment for his youthful misdemeanours and crimes, for which his mother had always excused him. It is possible, then, to identify some links between Nnamabia's decisions and his fate.

Q Who is the central character in this story: Nnamabia or the narrator (his unnamed sister)? Why?

Q How does this story set the tone for the rest of the collection?

Q Do you think Nnamabia's punishments match his crimes?

Imitation (pp.22–42)

Summary: *Nkem, living in America, discovers that her husband, Obiora, is having an affair in Nigeria; she reminisces about her past relationships with married men and her pride upon marrying and moving to America; Obiora arrives in America and she tells him that they are moving back to Lagos.*

The setting in 'Imitation' moves from Nigeria to America. Nkem's is the first of many stories of immigrant experience as a Nigerian American. These stories observe differences between the countries' cultures and detail the challenges of embracing a new world while maintaining beliefs and values of an old world. They also explore the often ambivalent feelings associated with immigration – many characters both appreciate and resent the lives imposed upon them by their adoptive homes.

Although 'Imitation' primarily concerns Nkem's relationship with her husband and her reaction to the news of his unfaithfulness, Nkem's processing of her husband's behaviour is grounded in her Nigerian upbringing, and also in the perspective of her Nigerian friends. The story, more broadly, is about the experience of living as a Nigerian in America.

A recurring motif is Nkem's perception of American culture and identity, including the following:

- The optimistic delivery man exhibits 'the abundance of unreasonable hope' (p.26) that characterises the country.
- Nkem likes the 'plastic' (p.24) lives of her neighbours, so foreign to her and far from the African poverty in which she was raised.
- She thinks America 'forces egalitarianism' (p.29), a conclusion she comes to while maintaining a friendship with her housegirl, Amaechi.
- Although she misses home, she has embraced American culture – she delights in baking cookies for her children's classes; 'America has grown on her' (p.37).

The central issue in 'Imitation' is the way Nkem responds to her husband's affair, but the text suggests that the distinction between right and wrong is not simple. Nkem 'is not so sure' about how she should react or feel (p.35), and we discover that she, when single, had relationships with married men. Neither she nor her husband is portrayed as 'good' or 'bad', and Adichie does not explicitly judge their infidelities. For example, Nkem's friend Ijemamaka and her housegirl argue that Obiora is 'a good man' (p.22 and p.35) who still loves his wife.

Key point

As a single woman, Nkem dated married men: '[W]hat single girl in Lagos hadn't?' (p.31). This hints at the cultural normality of the behaviour, helping to contextualise not only Obiora's affair, but also similar infidelities in later stories.

Q What is the significance of Obiora's gift (an Ife bronze head) in the story – for once, not an imitation but a genuine object?

A Private Experience (pp.43–56)

Summary: *When a riot breaks out in a marketplace, a Hausa Muslim and an Igbo Christian (Chika) shelter in an abandoned store; both women were separated from family members during the riot; Chika leaves but returns, injured; the next morning they leave and part company.*

After the 'plastic' (p.24) America of the last story, we are returned to a violent, volatile Africa – specifically the large northern city of Kano, with a majority population of Hausa people.

Chika is studying at the University of Lagos (approximately 1000 kilometres by road from Kano), and is in Kano with her sister, Nnedi, to visit their aunt. Chika lost Nnedi in the market when the riot began, and the unnamed Hausa woman directed Chika to the abandoned store, knowing it would be safe. While the violent ethnic and religious conflict takes place outside, Chika and the woman find some common experiences (such as losing family members in the marketplace) and, in the darkness, share compassion for each other while waiting out the night.

Key point

Chika's internal monologue (pp.43–4) illustrates some of the visual cues people use to categorise others: for example, Chika guesses the woman's ethnic identity from her facial features, and her religion based on her scarf. She thinks that the woman will similarly use complexion and jewellery to establish Chika's identity.

While there is little direct action in the story, the narrative regularly flashes forward to tell us how the experience will impact on Chika, and what she will come to understand. For example, 'Later, Chika will learn that, as she and the woman are speaking, Hausa Muslims are hacking down Igbo Christians with machetes' (p.44) and 'She will not find Nnedi' (p.47). The tension between the violent descriptions of the marketplace and the static energy within the store serves to heighten the impact of the events we do not actually witness.

This narrative technique privileges us with information to which the characters do not yet have access, allowing us to interpret deeper meaning in the story rather than simply engaging with the characters' immediate experiences. It offers an interesting contrast with the title of the story, which describes not just the Hausa woman's crying (p.51) and prayer (p.52), but also the two women's private – yet shared – experience of sheltering from danger. While their experience is indeed private, the story offers a broader point about how political difference is powerful and can be fatal, but need not always dictate interpersonal relations.

Near the end of the story, Chika realises that in the midst of violence, she and the Hausa woman have harboured no enmity: she will later 'remember that she examined the nipples and experienced the gentleness of a woman who is Hausa and Muslim' (p.55). The two, far from echoing the violent conflict demonstrated in the riot, show compassion for each other completely independent of their ethnic and religious identities and loyalties.

Key vocabulary

General Abacha: A military dictator, Sani Abacha was President of Nigeria from 1993 (when he took over the government in a coup) until his death in 1998.

Q Why do you think Chika lies about her mother (p.51)?

Q How do you think this experience might change both women?

Q What are the benefits of using visual cues to categorise others? What are the dangers?

Ghosts (pp.57–73)

Summary: *A retired academic visits the university to request his long-overdue pension; he converses with fellow past employees, recalling events and experiences from the Nigerian Civil War; he almost reveals to his former colleague Ikenna that his wife's ghost visits him regularly.*

James Nwoye, while at his former university, runs into a colleague he has for many years thought dead – killed, he believed, during the Nigerian Civil War. As the men tell each other what has happened in their lives since they last met, the reminiscences James describes are related to the Nigerian federal attack on Biafra, and specifically to when the town of Nsukka was taken.

The whole story has a sense of the 'hazy nostalgia' James experiences when discussing postwar lives with Ikenna (p.65). The imagery throughout conjures sad abandonment and the passing of time. Examples include:

- descriptions of the tired, 'dried-up-looking' clerks at the Bursary offices (p.57)
- the 'dry winds' of the *harmattan* season (p.59)
- the whirling dust (p.65 and p.71) and wind in the trees
- the worn leather and peeled paint in James' study.

These images convey the regret, resignation and sadness with which James seems to live his life, reflecting on the days when his friends and colleagues were young and energetic and prepared to do all they could for the Biafran cause. However, even the past is tinted with sorrow and regret. For example, James recalls he and his wife visiting their home after the Nigerian troops had left and the war had ended, and again the imagery is full of emptiness: they found the 'landscape of ruins' (p.65) so devastating that instead of staying to rebuild their lives, they moved to America for six years.

The title, too, echoes a pervasive nostalgia: the notion of 'ghosts' represents traces or memories of something (or someone) long gone and much missed. For example, while James mourns the loss of his wife, Ebere, Ikenna also mourns her, as a representation of 'a time immersed in possibilities' (p.66). Her ghost, for Ikenna, is the ghost of an era ended.

The central characters embody this sense of lost possibilities: Ikenna is 'a man who carries with him the weight of what could have been' (p.66), and James spends time 'thinking of the lives we might have had' (p.71).

This story also touches on issues common to others in the collection, including:

- the contrast between rich and poor (James' conditions in retirement, compared to those of the drivers and gardeners with whom he chats under the flame tree)
- sorrow over the directions that lives could have taken
- tension between the relative disadvantage of a life lived in Nigeria and one lived in America, as represented by James and Ebere's daughter Nkiru, who, in America, lives 'a life cushioned by so much convenience that it is sterile' (p.67) and calls home with her 'faint, vaguely troubling American accent' (p.71).

While there are a number of memorable events in the story (details of the war; Ebere's death, attributed to corruption and 'fake' drugs; the death of their first daughter, Zik; Ebere's ghostly visits to James), what is central is the tone of loss and sorrow, rather than the meaning or importance of specific incidents.

Key point

While James speaks both English and Igbo, on two occasions (p.64 and p.66) when he discusses the death of his loved ones, he insists on using Igbo, observing that to discuss death in English has 'a disquieting finality' (p.64). This reminds us that the differences between cultures are both pragmatic and subjective.

Adichie's father was also called James Nwoye, and her family lived in Nsukka, where he was a professor at the university. While this story is fictional, it contains many elements closely linked to Adichie's family history.

Key vocabulary

Harmattan: A dry north-easterly wind that blows between November and March, carrying dust and haze into West Africa.

Q Who are the 'ghosts' in this story?

On Monday of Last Week (pp.74–94)

Summary: *Kamara babysits seven-year-old Josh; she meets Josh's artist mother, Tracy, and is attracted to her, accepting an invitation to pose for her; in front of Kamara, Tracy also invites Josh's French teacher to pose.*

Like 'Imitation', this story presents the experience of a Nigerian woman finding her place in America, where she has come to live with her husband, Tobechi, after six years. Kamara took the job caring for Josh so that she might have 'a reason to leave the apartment every day' (p.79). While she has grown fond of him and his father, unlike Nkem in 'Imitation', Kamara feels mostly negative about her immigrant existence and about American culture. Even the accent sounds 'ungainly' (p.84) and 'false' (p.85) when her husband uses it, and 'American expressions' are 'clunky in her mouth' (p.75): she has not embraced her adopted nation. In her time with Josh she has learned from television 'how crazy these Americans were' (p.77).

When Kamara and Tobechi planned their move to America, they held a belief, like so many immigrants before and after, in 'the American dream': the idea that 'America was about hard work' (p.83), that wealth and accomplishment were available to all in this land of opportunity – a land where 'one would make it if one was prepared to work hard' (p.83). But reality contradicts this ideal. When Kamara finally joins Tobechi she is uncomfortable with the way he has assimilated into American culture (pp.84–6). In what is a recurring argument throughout this collection, we are presented with the notion that American wealth, far from being a welcome step up from a less privileged life in Nigeria, gives rise to fear and uncertainty. Kamara argues that 'a sated belly' (a symbol of wealth and success) not only makes Americans complacent, but also allows them the liberty of worrying about improbable disasters, meaning that parenting in America requires 'a juggling of anxieties' (p.82). The implication is that wealth facilitates misery, rather than alleviating it.

A second narrative thread is Kamara's imagined and hoped-for dalliance with Josh's mother. Tracy, an artist who seems to be mostly absent from her son's life, represents a freedom and a mystique far from Kamara's unsatisfying existence with Tobechi. When Kamara meets Tracy she is bewitched, and wildly imagines meetings of a more intimate nature; but when Tracy asks her to model, naked, for a painting, Kamara lacks confidence. She perhaps waits too long to accept the invitation, and Josh's French teacher replaces her in Tracy's sights. This recalls the nostalgia of James' thoughts on 'the lives we might have had' in 'Ghosts' (p.71), as well as illustrating the stark contrast between an imagined and a real life.

Q How do we know that Kamara feels isolated in America?

Q How does Kamara's immigrant experience differ from Nkem's? In what ways are their experiences similar?

Jumping Monkey Hill (pp.95–114)

Summary: *Ujunwa attends a writers' workshop organised by Edward Campbell, a former English lecturer, with writers from various African countries; they discuss the ways they are representing Africa; Ujunwa becomes uncomfortable with Edward's attentions; he says her story is not believable; she claims it is true.*

This story is explicit in its examination of the idea of Africa and an African identity. Edward Campbell, a British expert in African literature, has facilitated the workshop, gathering writers with a number of different perspectives on Africa, and these participants share their experiences of African identity socially and in workshopping their writing. Their representations of Africa are disputed, challenged and rejected by their fellow writers and, particularly, by Edward. Some of the broad questions raised by this story are:

- What *is* 'Africa'?
- What does it mean to be African?
- Is it possible to locate and represent a universal experience of Africa?

Edward is disappointed with much of the writing, not finding the answers for which he had hoped, as none of the stories offer him a universal experience of Africa, instead demonstrating that African identity is far from homogeneous (standardised and the same throughout) or easily summarised. When Edward criticises the stories for not representing 'Africa', he is projecting his expectations and perceptions of Africa; he does not recognise his own bias, even though he identifies and criticises such subjectivity in his writers. The Senegalese participant, for example, writes a story based on her experience of homosexuality, which – despite the evidence before him, in the form of the Senegalese woman's life – Edward dismisses as not being 'reflective of Africa' (p.108).

Key point

Ujunwa's response to Edward at this point is enlightening. She asks, 'Which Africa?' (p.108): a strong reminder that identity is complex, varied and subjective.

Ujunwa is the only writer referred to by her name, while the others are referred to by their nationality: the Ugandan, the Senegalese and so on. This suggests that the story is to be read broadly – even while the African writers are inherently subjective and individual, they also represent the experiences of larger groups of people. There is also irony in the fact that each writer, through their lack of an individual name, represents a whole country, and yet the central argument of the story is that identity is not homogeneous.

As well as exploring the notion of an African identity, the story explicitly analyses experiences of being a writer. For example, when Ujunwa is asked whether she is writing about her father, she denies it passionately, saying 'she had never believed in fiction as therapy' (p.103). And yet, her story clearly parallels life:

- Ujunwa's central character, Chioma, works in a bank; Ujunwa has just 'lost' her job in a bank (p.96) – or perhaps left it, as Chioma did (p.111).

- Chioma, too, wanted to be a writer from a young age.
- Ujunwa's father was the one who first encouraged her connection to literature (p.103); Chioma's father did the same thing (p.110).

In fact, at the conclusion of the story, she tells Edward and the others that nearly everything in her work is true. This raises questions about the nature of fiction:

- Ujunwa changes her claims to suit the circumstance – first the story is not about her father and then it is. Can authors be trusted to accurately disclose (or even recognise) the level of fiction in their work?
- Several of the workshop participants write about their experiences and are told by others that their stories are not believable – what does this suggest about the process of writing?
- Is fiction always 'some sort of therapy' (p.103)?
- Can fiction tell others' stories and experiences, or only the author's?

Key vocabulary

African Writers Series: A series of books by African writers, established in 1962. This series gave voice to African writers where colonial voices had dominated, aiming to redress an imbalance in the literature available for education. Under its first editor, Chinua Achebe, the series was prolific, but it declined in the late 1970s (indicating that this story is set after this period). In 'Jumping Monkey Hill', the writers' reference to the series (on p.102) helps contextualise their shared literary culture and background.

Alhaji: A title used in parts of West Africa to refer to a Muslim who has completed a pilgrimage to Mecca.

Q What does the story-within-a-story tell us about Ujunwa?

Q Whose Africa do we see in this story?

The Thing Around Your Neck (pp.115–27)

Summary: *Akunna wins an American visa lottery and moves from Lagos to Maine to live with an 'uncle'; he sexually harasses her so she leaves; she begins to work as a waitress and forms a relationship with a white American; the relationship struggles to overcome cultural differences; she eventually contacts her family, discovers her father has died and returns home.*

Like Nkem and Kamara in previous stories, Akunna finds that the reality of America does not live up to the dreams of her family back in Lagos. She finds the food nauseating (p.115), is shocked by the wastage (p.118) and the excess (p.124) and almost disappears in the anonymity of it all (p.119).

Akunna's aunts, uncles, cousins and friends in Nigeria are envious of her lottery visa, begging her to send gifts from America. Instead, after leaving her 'uncle', Akunna works hard for little money, sends half home to her parents, and can barely afford her rent, let alone an education, trips home or gifts. She is fiercely independent, having rejected the offer from her 'uncle' of financial support in exchange for sex. Similarly, when she enters into a cautious relationship with a young American man, she firmly rejects his offers to pay for them to visit Nigeria and, on hearing of her father's death, she returns alone.

This story is told in the unusual second-person narrative point of view, addressing the reader as if they were the central character. Readers of a second-person narrative are less inclined to question the decisions and behaviour of its central character, and more likely to engage with other themes and ideas in the text – in this case, perhaps the representation of American culture.

Q What do you think 'the thing around your neck' is? Where else in the collection can you identify the 'thing' referred to in the title of this story and the collection? (There may be many different answers.)

Q What might Akunna's two blank fortune-cookie strips (p.121) symbolise?

The American Embassy (pp.128–41)

Summary: *An unnamed woman queues at the American Embassy in Lagos to apply for asylum; she recalls the recent events that have led her there – her husband's 'disappearance' and her son's death; she attends a visa interview but walks out midway through it.*

As with other stories in the collection, events during the timeframe of the narrative are few; rather, the significant events occur in the time outside the story. In this case, it is the recent past that is the focus; we learn that the narrator's husband, a journalist, was persecuted for his pro-democracy, anti-Abacha articles. After he received an anonymous tip-off that he was in danger, she helped to smuggle him out via his sympathetic coeditor, and the next day three men invaded her house, in search of her husband, and accidentally shot her four-year-old son, Ugonna. These events are fresh in her mind as she enters the embassy to request asylum so that she may escape to America and join her husband.

During the interview her pride overcomes her: she realises that she would rather die before she 'hawked Ugonna for a visa to safety' (p.139). Yet without such details, she cannot prove that she is in danger. She knows that she will not be granted asylum and simply walks out of the embassy.

The story offers a glimpse into this woman's life in Nigeria during the Abacha regime. In the midst of national political unrest, the observations she makes are small and mundane – the fruits and vegetables for sale along the line to the embassy, what others are wearing, the conversations of those around her in the queue. Even the memories of her son's death are tinged with an everyday domesticity: she likens the blood from his gunshot wound to the palm oil she uses in her kitchen. This reminds us that while the impact of the war is far-reaching, and the conflict is on a national scale, the experiences of many of those living through it are situated in the everyday.

Q Do you think the woman's decision to protect her son's memory is heroic or foolish?

The Shivering (pp.142–66)

Summary: *A plane crash in Nigeria prompts two Nigerians (Chinedu and Ukamaka) in America to meet; Ukamaka tells Chinedu about her ex-boyfriend; they slowly form a friendship and Chinedu reveals that he too has lost a love; Chinedu confesses that his visa has expired; Ukamaka offers to help him.*

In the collection's longest story, several familiar themes are covered, including dynamics in male–female relationships (though the central one in 'The Shivering' is platonic) and the place of religion in contemporary life. A new theme, however, is hope. In the previous stories, there is a sense that the characters' lives have little possibility for change (except, perhaps, in 'Imitation', where Nkem ultimately takes charge of her destiny). Instead, the stories sketch the challenges characters face, portraying the sadness that many experience. In 'The Shivering', conversely, the sadness is primarily in the past (although Ukamaka is clinging defiantly to hers), and the story is about two characters finding their way forwards from failed relationships.

An example of the way this story's tone differs from others can be seen after Ukamaka learns that her ex-boyfriend, Udenna, was not on the flight that crashed. She cries 'from the relief of what had not happened and from the melancholy of what could have happened' (p.147). In 'The Shivering', though both Ukamaka and Chinedu are mourning the ending of relationships, the life they are experiencing is likely better than the lives they *might* have experienced, while in many other stories, the characters' lives are less fulfilling than those they think they could have led. The story ends on a much brighter note than many others in the collection, with images of hope, laughter and blessing.

Yet despite the hope, there are also dark undertones – such as in the impending threat of Chinedu's deportation – and the idea that women (and sometimes men, as in Chinedu's same-sex relationship) are dominated by their male partners and have little say in their lives.

Another important theme in this story is that of shared and differing religious experience. While Ukamaka and Chinedu first bond through prayer, this incident is also permeated by Ukamaka's discomfort with Chinedu's religious beliefs and style of worship; she is 'uneasy' (p.143) and longs for the praying to end. Their varying faiths continue to be an issue, though not causing significant conflict, and in the end they demonstrate that they can overcome this difference for the benefit of their friendship.

Q How do Chinedu's and Ukamaka's relationships with their ex-partners differ? In what ways are they alike? What does this tell you about the main characters' personalities?

Q What brings Chinedu and Ukamaka together? What maintains their friendship?

The Arrangers of Marriage (pp.167–86)

Summary: *Chinaza arrives in New York to her new home with her new husband; he attempts to assimilate her, forcing her to embrace American life; she becomes friends with Nia, a neighbour; she learns that her husband was previously married; she attempts to leave but returns the next night.*

Following the hopeful ending in 'The Shivering', we are immediately thrust back into the desperation and sadness of previous stories. From the title, we know that this story addresses lack of agency: Chinaza's life has already been determined by 'the arrangers of marriage', and she is now under the control of her new husband. All her life, she has had little say in what happens to her – from being denied the opportunity to go to university (p.171) to moving to America – and now that she is married, this looks set to continue.

The story catalogues the uninvited changes to Chinaza's life. From her name (her husband insists that she now use her English name, Agatha, and the English surname he has taken, Bell) to the way she has her tea, her new husband attempts to assimilate her into American culture, as he has done during more than a decade of living there. He insists that she:

- use American words for things – not only does he forbid her to use Igbo language in public (p.177) and in their home (p.178), but he corrects her British English to American, such as saying 'pitcher' instead of 'jug' (p.183)
- cook American food instead of traditional Nigerian meals, buying her an American cookbook (p.179)
- dress in American clothes he buys her (p.184).

The imagery and language help us to empathise with Chinaza and see America from her perspective: as unfamiliar and undesirable. For example, their new home is 'airless', 'old, musty' (p.167) and 'uncomfortable' (p.168); the air in the neighbourhood 'smelled of fish left out too long before refrigeration' (p.173) and, in the snow, the world outside is 'mummified into a sheet of dead whiteness' (p.186).

Chinaza's small attempts to take control of her life are always thwarted, leaving her dependent on a husband who seemingly has little affection for her, and appears bent on stripping away her sense of cultural identity, which is all she really has. No matter what she does, he is in control:

- She tries to buy a brand of biscuits she knows from home, to feel some small sense of familiarity and comfort, but he orders her to buy the cheaper generic brand (p.174).
- She is excited by the idea of securing employment and earning her own money, but her husband has no interest in following up her work permit (p.182).
- She begins to befriend Nia, finding stimulation and building some independence, but even this connection is tainted by her husband's power and influence; he had slept with Nia several years before (p.185).

Q How does Chinaza's experience of America differ from that of the women in other stories? What does it share with theirs?

Q Do you think Chinaza's husband, Ofodile (Dave), is living 'the American dream'?

Q Will Chinaza ever leave her husband? How does Adichie convince you of this?

Tomorrow Is Too Far (pp.187–97)

Summary: *The unnamed protagonist recalls her last summer in Nigeria and her brother's death; she returns eighteen years later, after her Grandmama's death; we discover that she was responsible for the death of her brother.*

This story explores a particular form of sibling rivalry: a girl desperate for her family's attention, resentful of her older brother, who is celebrated (particularly by his mother and grandmother) as the son who will inherit the family name. We see how he is spoiled and favoured and can do no wrong in his family's eyes, and we see the tragic result when his sister and their cousin attempt to 'make him less loveable ... Less able to take up ... space' (p.195). The impact of gender on the treatment of sons and daughters is alluded to, and the traditional cultural influence acknowledged, as Grandmama asserts that only her son's son, Nonso, can 'protect the family lineage' (p.189).

As with the title story, the narrative point of view is in the second person, again strongly encouraging us to align our sympathies with the protagonist. This is interesting, as the protagonist is responsible for the death of her brother, so we are being asked to accept her decisions and behaviour.

The Nigeria represented in this story is idyllic and bounteous – a childhood land of freedom, fruit trees, love and opportunity, where even the rain is 'silver' (p.189). Yet it is also a place of danger and unfulfilled promise – of snakes, death and the power of childhood resentment. While the moment before Nonso's accident was '[a]n open moment', vibrant with colour and possibility, with 'a sky washed clean' (p.196), his death fails to bring the attention, recognition and love the protagonist desires, instead taking her further from the Nigeria she loves, from her father and from any chance at happiness. Indeed, the final image is of the protagonist 'weeping, standing alone' (p.197). Just like many other moments in the collection, this description pulses with the regret of lost possibility, and of what could have been.

This story – with its idyllic garden, its deadly snake and its punishment of the central female character for her desires and actions – lightly echoes the biblical story of Eve in the garden of Eden.

Q How effective is the use of the second-person perspective in enabling us to sympathise with the central character?

The Headstrong Historian (pp.198–218)

Summary: *Nwamgba marries Obierika and has a son, Anikwenwa; Obierika dies; his cousins claim his land; missionaries arrive and Nwamgba sends Anikwenwa to learn English, hoping he can claim back the land; he comes to reject his Igbo identity; he marries and has a daughter, Grace, or Afamefuna, who will in the future become a historian.*

Nwamgba provides a direct contrast to the unnamed female character in the previous story. Nwamgba is headstrong and confident in her own abilities; as a child she wrestled her brother and won (p.199); as a young woman she makes a decision about whom she will marry; and once married she stands up to the bullies and gossips in the town. She also determines that she will take the future of the family into her hands by finding another wife for Obierika to increase his chances of producing offspring (p.200) – although this does not eventuate, and instead she defies the superstitions about Obierika's barren family tree and bears him a child. She is perceived by the white Catholic priest as 'troublingly assertive' (p.209).

The style and structure of this story also offer contrast with others in the collection. Where other stories focus on short periods of time ('Ghosts', 'On Monday of Last Week', 'Jumping Monkey Hill'), or even single events ('A Private Experience'), 'The Headstrong Historian' tells a bigger story, covering multiple generations and tracing the growing influence of white culture and religion in Nwamgba's Nigeria – as she ages, it is in 'a world that increasingly made no sense' (p.212).

White people in this story are missionaries, traders or slave dealers – all roles destined to change the routines, lives and fates of the Nigerians with whom they interact. The black Africans are described as 'normal men' (p.205), while the white men represent otherness, and the intrusion of an international community into traditional Nigerian customs, religion and expectations. Nwamgba resists the changes brought by the white people, yet sends her son to learn their ways, hoping that, in doing so, they will be able to stand up for their family's rights in the white courts. Unfortunately, her plan backfires when Anikwenwa embraces missionary values and religion, turning his back on Nwamgba's beliefs.

Key point

Nwamgba mourns yet another change, thinking it 'ludicrous how even the gods had changed and no longer asked for palm wine but for gin' (p.214) – a poignant illustration of the depth of the colonial impact on traditional cultures. The new beliefs and customs insinuate themselves even into existing traditions – in this case, consultation with the oracle.

Grace, Nwamgba's granddaughter, represents hope for the future, and a sense of regeneration of the old traditional ways that her father dismissed. We learn, in a future tense (just as we learn Chika's future in 'A Private Experience'), that she will study her ancestral and familial history, and eventually formally adopt the name her grandmother gave her, symbolising a new generation embracing a traditional pre-colonial culture.

Q What is the significance of the title of this story?

Q Why do you think Adichie places this story as the final one?

CHARACTERS & RELATIONSHIPS

Mothers

Key quotes

'[S]omebody had asked, "Which one is the mother?" and she had looked up, alert for a moment, and said, "I'm Ugonna's mother."' ('The American Embassy', pp.140–1)

'[S]he worried more than he did about their childlessness …' ('The Headstrong Historian', p.200)

Many of the central characters in the stories are mothers, and often their identity is tied up with their role as parents. For example, Nkem in 'Imitation' and the unnamed protagonist in 'The American Embassy' find purpose in their motherhood. Nkem's geographical location (which contributes to her identity) is determined by her responsibility to her children: she is sent to America for the birth of her first child, and she must remain there so the children can attend school, while her husband lives in Lagos.

Nkem has mixed feelings about this. At first she is proud to be part of 'the coveted league, the Rich Nigerian Men Who Sent Their Wives to America to Have Their Babies league' (p.26), and she is also proud that when she bakes for her children's classes, 'hers are always the favorites' (p.37). Her children give her life a focus while she lives away from her husband and her Nigerian culture, but it is not enough – she eventually asserts her needs and tells her husband that they are all moving home to Lagos. Yet even when she makes this announcement, she frames it in terms of the children: 'We have to find a school for Adanna and Okey in Lagos' (p.41). Her role as a mother has come to be central to her identity.

Similarly, in 'The American Embassy' the protagonist is attempting to escape from political persecution, but her focus is her recently murdered son, Ugonna. She has come to define herself in terms of her relationship to him: when he was born, he 'had given her a new life, surprised her by how quickly she took to the new identity he gave her, the new person he made her' (p.140). Her parental duty to protect him becomes so important to her that even after his death, she sacrifices her safety in order to avoid taking advantage of her son's memory.

'The Headstrong Historian' offers us another example of a woman primarily defined by her role as a mother. While Nwamgba has many other qualities (including determination, love for her husband and belief in her traditional customs), her most important role in the story is ultimately as Anikwenwa's mother. The narrative traces the decisions she has made about raising her son and their impacts upon his life, and indeed upon future generations of the family. While her motivation is often related to her love for Obierika, her actions are carried out in relation to their son. For example, in the hope of regaining Obierika's family land, she decides to send her son to learn English. This impacts on the rest of his life, and therefore on hers.

Even women who are not mothers are sometimes defined by their relationships to children. Kamara has no children, though she is shaped by her carer role with Josh. In addition, she wants a child; 'she resented those manicured women with their effortlessly conceived babies' (p.82) and begins 'willing herself to become pregnant, because if that did not shake her out of her dismay at least it would give her something to care about' (p.86). She longs for the identity-defining power of motherhood.

The text argues that identity can be constructed by familial roles (such as motherhood) and that women who are mothers cannot be independent of that responsibility; their children must shape their decisions and experiences.

Mothers who favour sons

The central characters in a number of stories are daughters rather than mothers, and hold resentment towards their mothers because of the preferential treatment towards sons. Stories in which this occurs include 'Cell One', 'Tomorrow Is Too Far' and, to a lesser extent, 'The Thing Around Your Neck' (with mention of the sons' schooling, p.118).

In 'Cell One', Nnamabia's mother consistently excuses his misbehaviour (for example, pp.6–7, p.15). His unnamed sister reveals some resentment for the extent of her mother's tolerance. When she stands up against her parents to say that they should not visit Nnamabia in jail every day, it is her mother whose fury she expects (p.14). We know little about her life except as it relates to her brother, and this helps to illustrate Adichie's argument that female Nigerian children often come second to their male siblings, and that mothers tend to heighten this inequity.

In 'Tomorrow Is Too Far', the imbalance in treatment between Nonso and his sister is even more marked, and both their grandmother and their mother are explicit about Nonso's superior role in the family. Their grandmother's explanation is that he will carry on the family name, and this justifies her favouring him in every way, even when his sister's skills are superior – for example, in tree-climbing (p.187, p.195). Their mother's favouritism is less clear, but she obviously enjoys her son's company more than her daughter's – for example, she never laughs with her daughter the way she does with her son (p.190).

Through characters and relationships such as these, the text suggests that there is discrimination embedded in some traditional gender roles within families, and that daughters may not be able to access the same support from their mothers that sons can.

A contrast is offered in 'Jumping Monkey Hill', where Ujunwa appears to have a close relationship with her mother. Perhaps this is partially because Ujunwa and her mother were united in supporting each other when Ujunwa's father had an affair (if Chioma's story does indeed reflect Ujunwa's). Perhaps, too, the absence of a brother in Ujunwa's life means that she does not need to compete for her mother's affections, and so their relationship is simpler.

Another contrast is offered by the easy relationship between Chika and her sister Nnedi – there is none of the competition illustrated in the male–female sibling relationships, and instead they are close and supportive.

Q Does the text argue that motherhood enhances or restricts a woman's identity?

Q What other sibling dynamics can you identify in the text?

Unfulfilled wives

Key quotes

'I had thanked them both for … finding me a husband … I did not remind them that I wanted to take the JAMB exam again and try for the university.' ('The Arrangers of Marriage', p.170)

'She walks out into the hallway, up the wide stairs, then back downstairs and into the kitchen … She would smell Obiora's closet, run her hand over his cologne bottles, and push suspicions from her mind.' ('Imitation', p.27)

While some marriages in the stories are happy, many are not. The text portrays a number of women who are disempowered in their marriages or relationships, feeling uncertain about their place in the world beyond their 'wifely duties' (p.168).

This is particularly notable with the Nigerian wives in America. There is a distinct sense that in immigrating with their husbands, these women have found themselves in an unfamiliar culture and environment, and they are often unsatisfied with their lives.

Note, however, that while there are multiple examples of wives with similar experiences, the collection does present evidence of women in other situations. Be careful not to generalise too broadly about the representations of types of characters throughout the text.

Nkem

Nkem, while she still loves her husband and does demonstrate her capacity to steer her own destiny when she tells him they will return to Lagos, often seems bewildered by her marriage and the life she 'never imagined' (p.27). Their American prosperity has allowed her the unenviable luxury of feeling disengaged. Her housegirl, Amaechi, is 'much better in the kitchen than she is' (p.33), leaving her nothing to do in that area. The children attend the school her husband chose, and she lives in the house her husband bought, while he spends most of the year back in Lagos (having, as she discovers, at least one affair).

Nkem empathises with imagined Benin servants – who once carried the original masks of which her gifts are imitations – 'wishing they had a say' (p.23). She awaits her unfaithful husband's visits and does things 'the way Obiora likes' (p.27). These qualities all suggest that Nkem is drifting, lacking purpose, not necessarily unhappy but very much disenfranchised from her own life.

Kamara

Like Nkem, Kamara married her husband, Tobechi, happily; we learn about their early relationship in Nigeria (p.83). But Kamara had to wait to join him in America and, like Nkem, she becomes disenchanted once in Philadelphia.

Kamara's job as nanny to Josh, while something she enjoys, is work she took at her husband's insistence and under his guidance. Yet at the same time, she knows she 'had not really needed to be persuaded. She wanted the job, any job; she wanted a reason to leave the apartment every day' (p.79). Without this work, her existence lacked purpose and direction. Like many of the mothers in the collection, Kamara's days become defined by her relationship to a child (Josh) and, by extension, to his father (Neil). Finally, this connection extends to Josh's mother Tracy, but while Kamara is drawn to her, she does not act immediately on Tracy's invitation to pose for her. Instead she lacks confidence in herself and her rights and responsibilities beyond her marriage, and is ultimately unable to pursue an opportunity she desires.

Chinaza

Chinaza, more strongly than any of the other characters, embodies the notion that the life of a married Nigerian woman in America is unfulfilling. Her story suggests that immigration, far from offering a wife the new life of opportunity that America is so often portrayed as providing, brings only disillusionment, loneliness and restriction.

When she arrives at her new home (a small flat instead of the house she had been led to expect), she is lonely, unprepared for her role as a wife and completely under her husband's control – from the financial limits regarding what she is allowed to spend on phone calls or even biscuits to the ways she must reject her Nigerian identity and embrace an American one. A deep sense of sadness pervades her new life; her surroundings are gloomy, and she has little hope of stimulation or expansion. Yet, she knows there is little at home for her if she were to leave (pp.184–5). Although Nia's last words to her are encouraging, the text suggests that such hope for future opportunities is denied Nigerian immigrant wives.

Ukamaka

Although not married to Udenna, Ukamaka experienced similar dynamics in her relationship, and the text suggests that her life might have followed a similar trajectory to that of the other married women. For example, even after he has left, she still cooks food in the way that Udenna preferred: 'I never liked hot food until I met Udenna. I'm not even sure I like it now' (p.151).

Q Can you identify any wives in the collection who present an alternative perspective on marriage?

Unnamed African women

Key quotes

'She sat there for a long time ... trying to decide whether to name her character something common, like Chioma, or something exotic, like Ibari.' ('Jumping Monkey Hill', p.100)

'Nobody knew where you were, because you told no one. Sometimes you felt invisible ...' ('The Thing Around Your Neck', p.119)

The first quotation above, from Ujunwa, the writer, reminds us how important names are, and how carefully authors consider these decisions. A name can convey a great deal of information about a character, and can serve as a shortcut for readers, suggesting details such as cultural background, as well as hinting at personality. To leave a character unnamed, then, is an equally powerful decision.

In several of the stories, the central characters remain nameless. This suggests that Adichie wishes them to represent something beyond the individual experience of their particular lives. For example, in 'The American Embassy' the unnamed wife of the political journalist represents the many women in her position: endangered by the actions of their husbands or families. She also represents the mourning mothers of the many children who have been killed in civil war and unrest in Nigeria. While her son, Ugonna, is named, she remains almost anonymous, and thus her experience could be that of any mother.

In 'Cell One' and 'Tomorrow Is Too Far', the central characters are also unnamed young women. However, their brothers (who play very important roles in the narratives) are named, suggesting that within the family dynamics, and perhaps also in broader community perceptions of identity, sons are more significant than daughters.

The anonymity of these women also suggests that many young Nigerian women are often at the mercy of others – of husbands, families, society at large – and do not have power over their destinies or even identities. They are defined by their relationships to others, whether they be sisters, wives or mothers, and their experiences reflect the experiences of other unnamed women just like them.

Q Do the stories with unnamed central characters differ in any way from those whose protagonists have names? (Think about style, subject matter and themes.)

Men

Key quotes

'You will forgive him, madam. Men are like that.' ('Imitation', p.34)

'If you let him, he would do many things for you.' ('The Thing Around Your Neck', p.117)

'If he thought I was too happy about something that did not have to do with him, he always found a way to put it down.' ('The Shivering', p.153)

Although the central characters in the majority of these stories are female, there are significant male characters in their lives, and some stories – 'Ghosts' and, arguably, 'Cell One' – feature male protagonists.

The men in *The Thing Around Your Neck* are nearly all husbands and fathers, or brothers. Very few move through the world independently of such ties. Exceptions are Chinedu (a recently single gay man) and Dozie (a cousin of, and potential love interest for, the unnamed protagonist of 'Tomorrow Is Too Far'). Anikwenwa, in 'The Headstrong Historian', is an only child, but his role in the story becomes most important once he is a father to Grace, or Afamefuna. Like the women, then, the men in the stories are often defined by their roles in their families.

The focus on familial roles in the text suggests that individual identity may be less important than interpersonal relationships.

Husbands and brothers

Most men in the stories are young husbands or brothers to the central female characters. On the whole, the men are not presented in an admirable light, often serving as restrictive, dominant (even if gentle and well-meaning) and disempowering figures in the women's lives. Many of these men share personality traits and qualities. These include being:

- ambitious and often driven in terms of career, wealth and status – for example, 'We will live in a house like that one day' (Tobechi, p.83) or 'when I become an Attending, we will not live in a neighborhood like this' (Ofodile, p.175)

- rebellious and volatile – particularly Nnamabia, but to some extent the boyfriend in 'The Thing Around Your Neck', and Ikenna (in both his own and others' recollections)
- self-righteous and filled with a sense of entitlement – especially Anikwenwa, and both Ukamaka's and Chinedu's ex-boyfriends
- confident in their roles (particularly within marriages) and often not prepared to consider the feelings or needs of their sisters, daughters or wives.

The text suggests that within male–female relationships of all kinds, young men often hold the balance of power.

Fathers

Many of the older men in the text are fathers or father figures. For example, Edward, in 'Jumping Monkey Hill', plays a fatherly role among the group of writers, having gathered them together and holding the power over the workshop process, as well as exercising a form of emotional power when he issues his authoritative pronouncements on each of their works. Edward also holds sexual power over the female writers in the group, shown when, despite being married, he flirts with Ujunwa (p.106) and the Senegalese woman (p.111).

Other controlling fathers in the text include:

- Obiora in 'Imitation' (the decisions about the children are largely his, despite his being in Nigeria most of the time)
- Chioma's father, who perhaps represents Ujunwa's father, in 'Jumping Monkey Hill' (Chioma's only path to employment is through her father's influence with the banks)
- Neil in 'On Monday of Last Week' (while not the father of a daughter, and while he cares deeply for his son, he is still extremely controlling in his role as parent).

There are also some fathers in the text who are relatively benign, such as Nnamabia's father ('Cell One'), James ('Ghosts') and Obierika ('The Headstrong Historian'). These characters are more incidental and less important to their respective narratives.

James, Chinedu and Dozie

Chinedu and Dozie are exceptions in the text because their relationships with female characters are not primarily defined by sexual or gender-based power – though Dozie's relationship to the protagonist in 'Tomorrow Is Too Far' is of a romantic nature. Nor are they fathers, and in their respective stories they serve as positive figures in the females' lives. James, while a father, is not defined by this role, and instead serves as a nostalgic representation of a time gone by.

Although Dozie is a love interest for the unnamed female protagonist in 'Tomorrow Is Too Far', this relationship never eventuates and is always secondary in the text to the protagonist's relationship with her brother.

Chinedu, by virtue of his homosexual orientation, is simply a platonic friend for Ukamaka – the dynamic between them is not influenced by sexual politics (though Ukamaka briefly considers an affair with him before discovering that he is gay). Through his relationship with Abidemi, Chinedu helps to reinforce the notion that traditional male roles encompass power over partners. Even though, in this case, Abidemi's partner is also male, Abidemi exhibits the same power over Chinedu that other husbands exhibit over their wives in these stories.

Q Does the text suggest that gender roles are determined by traditional cultural norms?

Q What does the text suggest about characters who transgress traditional power balances?

THEMES, IDEAS & VALUES

Cultural identity

Key quotes

'It is what America does to you … It forces egalitarianism on you.' ('Imitation', p.29)

'Edward chewed his pipe thoughtfully before he said that homosexual stories of this sort weren't reflective of Africa, really. "Which Africa?" Ujunwa blurted out.' ('Jumping Monkey Hill', p.108)

'… America was give-and-take. You gave up a lot but you gained a lot, too.' ('The Thing Around Your Neck', p.116)

'They will never move forward unless they adapt to America.' ('The Arrangers of Marriage', p.175)

The idea of African (usually Nigerian) identity is central to most of these stories, and particularly those set in America, where the immigrant Nigerian characters have the opportunity to view their culture from a distance, and, by comparison with their adoptive culture, to assess its values and impacts on individuals. The stories also examine notions of multiple micro cultures within Africa, and particularly Nigeria – as defined by race, class or religion.

Being Nigerian in Africa

Many of the stories portray experiences of being a Nigerian in Nigeria. (These individuals are primarily Igbo and often Christian, but some belong to other ethnic/religious groups, such as Hausa Muslim.) We see the impact of Nigerian culture – from traditional gender roles to cuisine – on individuals in various areas of the community, such as the academic context of the university, during the last fifty years.

Stories such as 'Cell One', 'A Private Experience', 'Ghosts' and 'The American Embassy' illustrate the day-to-day impact of civil unrest, violence and war in a volatile country. Conflicts are political, racial and religious. In 'Cell One', the 'cults', as well as the fights and the killings on campus and in the jails, appear to be the generic result of living in a country with a history of violence. These acts have no clear cause but the culture of corruption (exemplified in the jail) and the pervasive influence of the civil war. As Chika observes in 'A Private Experience', 'riots do not happen in a vacuum' (p.48) and individual behaviour is strongly shaped by context.

Other stories, such as 'The Headstrong Historian', explore more domestic experiences of Nigerian life, such as visiting an oracle, communicating with the Women's Council, collecting clay and herbs, attending coming-of-age ceremonies such the *ima mmuo* and preparing and eating traditional foods.

Most of the stories in the collection generally offer an *implicit* examination of what it means to be Nigerian: cultural identity is an aspect of the text, but it is not overtly discussed. In contrast, 'Jumping Monkey Hill' and 'The Headstrong Historian' provide meta-reflections on, respectively, the notion of an 'African identity' and the impact of colonial intrusion in traditional Nigerian culture. These stories *explicitly* examine what it means to be Nigerian or African, articulating these questions within the narrative. Examples include:

- the writers' conversation about national characteristics of people from different African cultures, and about literary representations of African culture (p.102)
- the discussions between Edward and the writers about what constitutes contemporary African experience (pp.107–8; pp.113–14)
- Ujunwa's accusation that the 'Black South African' is exhibiting a national attitude that was a contributing factor in South Africa's apartheid history (p.112)
- the Anglican teacher's rationalisation about how colonial teaching within traditional cultures should occur (p.209)
- Grace's studies of Nigerian history (p.215, p.217) and her 'reimagining the lives and smells' of her forebears (p.217).

Key point

The text argues that while national or cultural experiences of African-ness can contribute significantly to individuals' identity, there is no one representative or definitive model of what it means to be African or Nigerian.

Immigration: being Nigerian in America

Another way that the text explores the notion of cultural identity is by focusing on characters who are displaced – removed from their traditional backgrounds, families and traditions – and resettled within a new culture. The immigrant stories in *The Thing Around Your Neck* examine American culture from an outsider's perspective, offering us both an illustration of American identity and, through the juxtaposition of the two cultures, another representation of Nigerian identity.

Female Nigerian immigrants, mainly new wives, characterise America as:

- a place with people who have an 'abundance of unreasonable hope' (Nkem, p.26)
- a 'country of curiosities and crudities, this country where you could drive at night and not fear armed robbers, where restaurants served one person enough food for three' (Nkem, p.37)
- a place where 'having too much food' and 'luxury' (Kamara, p.82) can lead to an inflated sense of power, such as the conviction that parents can protect their children completely
- a world where you could 'buy presents that were just presents and nothing else, nothing useful' (Akunna, p.124).

The unnamed protagonist in the title story emigrates to America on her family's fantasies of a country where everyone has 'a car and a gun' and even new immigrants can have 'a big car' and 'a big house' (p.115). The visa interviewer in 'The American Embassy' also claims that 'The United States offers a new life' to those legitimately escaping the violence of Nigeria under General Abacha's rule (p.140).

The America constructed in these stories is one of excess, wealth, privilege and potential. Those immigrants who have established lives there are still working towards 'the American dream', doing everything they can to embrace their new culture and reap the fabled benefits of this land of opportunity.

In contrast, Adichie's Nigeria is one where violence, poverty and struggle are part of everyday life. Examples are numerous, and include:

- the prevalence of violence in 'Cell One' – 'Cult wars had become common' (p.7) and '[i]t was so abnormal that it quickly became normal' (p.8), and within the jail, being 'in trouble' (p.11) is serious; when a man dies in a neighbouring cell, the policemen exhibit him as a warning to others (p.12)
- the violent riot in 'A Private Experience', which is not an isolated event
- the story Akunna tells of her father's struggle to earn a sufficient income (p.122)
- the corruption preventing old men from receiving pensions in 'Ghosts', as well as the descriptions of the civil war and its aftermath (e.g. p.63)
- the persecution, poverty and desperation of the many Nigerians in 'The American Embassy'.

'The American Embassy' crystallises the notion of the desirability of escaping Nigeria for America. Every day that the Embassy opens, hundreds of people line up before dawn for a chance to apply for visas; the number of potential immigrants well exceeds the volume the embassy can (or is willing to) process. Many Nigerians long for a new life and even a new cultural identity.

What does the text imply, then, about an immigrant experience? Although it compares two cultures, it is not an argument for the value of one over the other. Despite the number of Nigerians wanting to emigrate to America, many of the successful immigrant characters observe that with wealth and comfort comes a host of negative consequences; with sanitisation and excess can come a loss of value and integrity. Instead, the collection presents an exploration of the impact of leaving one's home. As Nkem reluctantly acknowledges of America and Nigeria, 'When you've been here so long, you're not the same, you're not like the people there' (p.29), suggesting that embracing one culture can mean relinquishing another.

Q How do the Nigerian characters in Africa differ from the Nigerians in America?

Marriage and relationships

Key quotes

'When he asked if she would marry him, she thought how unnecessary it was, his asking, since she would have been happy simply to be told.' ('Imitation', p.32)

'"Staid" was the word he had used ... Staid, and yet she had been arranging her life around his for three years.' ('The Shivering', p.148)

'... it was better that he let her go with the man she chose, to save himself years of trouble when she would keep returning home after confrontations with in-laws.' ('The Headstrong Historian', p.199)

As discussed in 'Characters & Relationships', in this text the gender roles in marriages (as well as in other male–female relationships) tend to follow a similar pattern: females are financially and emotionally at the mercy of their fathers, brothers or husbands.

Many of the central characters in these stories are young women, and approximately half are married. Overwhelmingly, the marriages are not happy ones – while the women may not be in crisis, many feel isolated or trapped in their relationships. Even when the marriage was by choice, as in the cases of Nkem or Kamara, the wives are subservient and often have little power in their day-to-day or long-term lives.

The text suggests that marriage is often not an ideal for young Nigerian women, but a fate determined by others, and one to be endured. There is the implication that this reflects traditional gender roles and power dynamics, but this is not explicitly stated. Stories like 'The Arrangers of Marriage' illustrate for readers the practice of marrying young women without their consultation, but in other stories it is not so simple. Nkem, for example, was pleased to accept Obiora's proposal, but she does note that she would have been 'happy simply to be told' (p.32), suggesting that she comes from a background where a woman does not expect to have a choice when it comes to marriage.

The text does not offer us much insight into the males' feelings about marriage, since the central characters are usually wives rather than husbands. Even when we do have access to the male characters' emotional experiences, we tend not to learn how they feel about their marriages; for example, Neil's thoughts and feelings tend to relate to his role as Josh's father, rather than his relationship with Tracy.

Even the incidental relationships and marriages in the collection, such as that of Nnamabia's parents, do not necessarily seem very happy (they disagree over parenting decisions). The protagonist's parents in 'Tomorrow Is Too Far' are divorced, and Chioma's parents (and perhaps Ujunwa's) in 'Jumping Monkey Hill' separate too.

Happily ever after?

Even in the stories where the marriages were once successful, usually one spouse is now absent, suggesting that married bliss cannot last forever even if it does occur. While the text argues that love and happiness are valuable and desirable, it implies that they cannot by themselves overcome the challenges of everyday life, and that they are far from permanent or unchanging. The unions in the following stories illustrate this:

- 'Ghosts' – James' wife Ebere has passed away (though James does still derive some comfort from her ghostly presence).
- 'The American Embassy' – the unnamed protagonist has lost not only her son, but also her husband, who has presumably escaped to a new life of freedom in America. The story suggests that she will not follow him, and probably will never see him again.
- 'The Shivering' – Ukamaka spends most of her time mourning a relationship, suggesting she was once happy. However, all her recollections suggest that the relationship was imperfect, and certainly it was not lasting.

- 'The Headstrong Historian' – from early in the story, Nwamgba is mourning her beloved Obierika, and even seeks to find his reincarnated spirit in her grandchildren. Like James who is comforted by Ebere's ghostly presence, Nwamgba finds comfort when she senses Obierika's presence in her granddaughter, but this comfort is only a pale shadow of her past happiness.

Infidelity

A common motif in many of the stories is the infidelity of husbands; occasionally women consider infidelity too. Examples include:

- Obiora, who has an ongoing affair with a woman in Lagos
- the married men with whom Nkem had relationships while she was single
- Kamara, who, while she doesn't ultimately act on her desires with Tracy, considers it
- the husband of Kamara's friend Chinwe
- Chioma's father (and, by extension, perhaps Ujunwa's father)
- the protagonist's 'uncle' in 'The Thing Around Your Neck', who attempts to initiate a relationship with her while living with his wife and family
- possibly the American boyfriend in 'The Thing Around Your Neck'; when the waiter at Chang's asks if he has a girlfriend in Shanghai, he 'smiled and said nothing' (p.123)
- Abidemi, who becomes engaged to Kemi while with Chinedu; his intention to carry on his relationship with Chinedu, even after he marries, demonstrates a willingness to cheat on both boyfriend and wife
- Ofodile (Dave), who did not tell Chinaza he was already married – even though 'just on paper' (p.183)
- Ayaju suggests that Nwamgba take a lover, as 'other women in her situation did' (p.201), in order to provide the heir that her husband was struggling to produce.

The frequency with which infidelity occurs in the text suggests that it is, to some extent, an established cultural behaviour. Several stories also acknowledge the right for men to take more than one wife (for example, the husband of Kamara's friend Chinwe takes another wife, and Nwamgba considers finding a second wife for Obierika). This might appear to be a form of infidelity from the perspective of cultures where polygamy is not morally or legally acceptable, including America and Australia. However, polygamy is not presented as infidelity in the text, and the way in which a reader responds to such relationships is an example of how cultural bias might colour an interpretation. The text does not offer a value judgement on polygamy, although readers might.

The polygamy mentioned in 'On Monday of Last Week' and 'The Headstrong Historian' suggests a culture of acceptance of wandering affections, at least for males. This might partially explain the high incidence of infidelity among characters in these stories. In a culture where males may marry more than one wife, the infidelity of married men might not be seen in quite the same moral light as in a country such as Australia, where monogamy is largely the accepted marital state and the legal, if not ethical, model.

Although it is not discussed in depth, passing mentions inform us that while infidelity may be accepted or at least tolerated in some Nigerian circles, there are rules about how it should occur. Some of the men flout these rules, and it seems that these transgressions – rather than the infidelity itself – are what the text critiques. For example, it is assumed that Obiora has affairs in Lagos, but it is when he brings the girlfriend into his marital home that the relationship becomes the subject of gossip and he is judged to have '[n]o respect' (p.22). Adichie suggests that transgression of societal rules is unacceptable. As readers, we should be careful to note what these rules are, as presented in the stories, and not assume that they align with our own.

However, while society might accept the infidelity of husbands, the text does also suggest that the women whose husbands are unfaithful suffer because of it. For example, Chinaza is distressed on discovering Ofodile's previous marriage, even though her marriage is not based on love or choice. Similarly, Obiora's infidelity is what prompts Nkem's pronouncement that they will return to Lagos. *The Thing Around Your*

Neck, as well as demonstrating an accepted cultural norm, manages to critique it subtly by demonstrating the impact of infidelity on the wives.

Q How would you describe any difference between polygamy and infidelity? Does the text differentiate between the two?

Religion

Key quotes

'"Have faith" was like saying be tall and shapely.' ('The Shivering', p.148)

'She knows the woman is on her knees, facing Mecca, but she does not look. It is like the woman's tears, a private experience, and she wishes that she could ... believe in a god.' ('A Private Experience', p.52)

Religion is ever-present in these stories, whether in the foreground or the background. Religious affiliation is often a point of difference between characters, such as Chika and the Hausa woman ('A Private Experience'), Ukamaka and Chinedu ('The Shivering') and Anikwenwa and Nwamgba ('The Headstrong Historian'). In other stories, such as 'Cell One', religion is simply an element of the characters' lives that is taken for granted.

The collection suggests that religion is a central part of Nigerian existence. Even when characters do not discuss or practise a particular religion, they are aware of it in their surroundings. For example, when the protagonist of 'The American Embassy' observes those around her, she notices beggars 'who fingered prayer beads and quoted the Koran' or wore 'blue medals of the Blessed Virgin Mary hanging around their necks' (p.137). She catalogues such details just as she might mention what someone was wearing, reminding us that religious faith of some kind is the cultural norm.

Religious difference

In the broad landscape of these stories, religious difference is responsible for conflict and violence, such as in the riots in 'A Private Experience'.

But in the more domestic sphere, Adichie shows characters attempting to respect one another's differences, recognising similarities and showing compassion and tolerance.

'A Private Experience' offers a strong example of this. While religious difference outside the store is leading to extreme violence, inside, the Christian woman observes a respectful silence and distance while the Muslim woman prays (pp.51–2), even feeling 'strangely energized' (p.52) afterwards. In turn, the Hausa woman, far from judging Chika on religious grounds, continues to offer her protection and support, such as when Chika is injured (p.54). The two exchange sympathies, blessings and hopes for their respective family members who are missing, putting aside their differences to show basic kindness to each other. This story demonstrates that religious difference can be overcome, at least on a small scale, and that diversity is to be respected. The story also argues that cooperation and tolerance are to be valued: they lead to the survival of both women, while outside, in the midst of religious conflict, many lives are lost.

A tolerance for differences of belief is also demonstrated in 'The Shivering', although perhaps not as explicitly. An important theme in this story is religion: Ukamaka goes to the Catholic Church (although she feels disillusioned, no longer experiencing the faith she held strongly as a teenager), and Chinedu is a passionate member of the Pentecostal community. They respect each other's different connections to religion, and Ukamaka often questions Chinedu about his faith – a level of religious belief she can no longer find for herself (for example, pp.164–5). Structurally, Adichie demonstrates that religion is a central theme in the story, as key elements of the narrative are tied to religious experience. For example:

- the beginning – the main characters meet through religion (Chinedu comes to Ukamaka's apartment so they can pray together)
- the conclusion – they reconcile after their argument, strengthen their friendship, and share a hopeful and positive experience while attending the Catholic Church

- the title – this refers to Ukamaka's unexplained physical sensation while they are praying (p.144; they also reflect back on it, p.164).

In this story, Adichie demonstrates that by overcoming their religious difference, the two are able to form a lasting connection that offers them support and companionship. Again, the text argues for the value of tolerance and for individuals' rights to choose their own faith and beliefs.

Questioning religion

While the collection argues that it is normal to have some connection with a particular religion, and that acceptance of others' beliefs is to be valued, it does not suggest that faith is straightforward. Several characters question their religious beliefs and values, and the text does not draw a moral conclusion about this, rather suggesting that religion can be a very different experience for each individual. Characters who have conflicted relationships with religion include:

- Chika and her sister Nnedi. Nnedi scorns her mother's faith, refusing to wear a rosary. Chika is more equivocal – she has no strong religious belief, envying the Hausa woman her ability to 'believe in a god, see an omniscient presence in the stale air of the store' (p.52). She wears a finger rosary only to please her mother, but after her experience during the riot and after losing her sister, she will 'change her mind about telling her mother that offering Masses is a waste of money' (p.52), tentatively finding a new role in her life for the comforts of religion.
- Ukamaka, who is embarrassed by Chinedu's dramatic prayer and demonstrative faith, and regularly questions the logic of God and the place of religion in her existence.
- Anikwenwa, who is raised in one religion and educated in another, and must face difficult decisions about which to follow. For example, he does not wish to participate in a traditional initiation ceremony (pp.210–11), and insists that his wife Mgbeke (Agnes) not attend her Anglican friend's wedding (p.213).
- Agnes – while she has adopted Christianity and doesn't actively question it – is caught between cultures. For example, she seeks

solace in Nwamgba, but is fearful when Nwamgba tries to include her in a traditional custom (consulting the oracle). Similarly, she tries to join other women at the traditional sacred Oyi waters but keeps her clothes on, trying to maintain her 'Christian decency'.

All of these characters struggle with religion as they struggle with other parts of their lives, such as personal relationships and connections to cultures. This suggests that religion, like love and ethnicity, can form a significant part of our identity.

Q Does religion offer anything positive for the characters in these stories? Give examples to support your answer.

Q Do you think many of the characters in *The Thing Around Your Neck* have a choice about their religious connections?

Disempowerment and agency

Key quotes

'Suddenly, she can't remember anything, can't remember where her life has gone.' ('Imitation', p.40)

'She had not planned to say it, but it seems right, it is what she has always wanted to say.' ('Imitation', p.41)

'You were used to accepting what life gave, writing down what life dictated.' ('The Thing Around Your Neck', p.121)

The text argues that when individuals lack agency (the power or ability to make decisions and act on them) in their lives, they are left with little hope or positivity. Many of the characters – particularly, but not exclusively, the women – are disempowered and do not have the means to direct their lives. Sometimes this power has been removed externally, such as when Chinaza is sent to a new life with a new husband in a new country. In other cases, characters such as Akunna simply do not know how to take control: she 'did not know … that people could dictate to life' (p.121).

Few of the stories portray their protagonists as content with their lives. Rather, they are often suffering, whether through the loss of loved ones (as in 'A Private Experience', 'Ghosts', 'The American Embassy', 'The Shivering', 'The Headstrong Historian' and perhaps even 'Tomorrow Is Too Far'), the loss of ideals or possibilities ('Cell One', 'Ghosts' and 'On Monday of Last Week') or a more general dissatisfaction with the way things are ('Imitation', 'Jumping Monkey Hill' and 'The Arrangers of Marriage').

In all these instances, a lack of control or agency can be seen as the cause of the suffering. If the characters had the means (confidence, finances, permission, knowledge or power) to change their circumstances, things would likely improve. For example, if Kamara felt capable of acting on her desire to pose for Tracy (with the implication that the desire is also at least partially sexual), she might find 'something to care about' (p.86), something to give her life focus and purpose.

Characters who lack agency

Nnamabia: The events in his life seem not to follow any logical path: certainly he has committed crimes, but his arrest is due to his being in the wrong place at the wrong time, and his release is equally attributed to random good fortune.

Nkem: Her life has been shaped by her husband's decisions, and her time in America is spent waiting for his visits. However, she demonstrates some agency at the end of the story when she determines that they will return to Lagos.

Chika: She is caught up in a riot with which she has little political involvement. She survives only because the Hausa woman happens to stop her as she runs past, redirecting her to the empty store.

Kamara: Her job was her husband's suggestion, and she is hesitant to make decisions to change her circumstances, as illustrated in her initial reluctance to accept Tracy's invitation to pose. Though she does eventually agree, she has no power to make the liaison happen; it is still up to Tracy to act.

Ujunwa/Chioma: Although Chioma is a character in a story-within-a-story, Ujunwa claims that Chioma's story is hers, and so we can perhaps read parallels between them. Ujunwa's employment – if we are to read her story as true – is dependent on her father and on the whims of the *alhaji*. Similarly, at the writers' workshop she is under Edward's influence and control. When she finds that she is not the only one he has sexually harassed, she wonders, 'But why do we say nothing?' (p.112), suggesting that all the women at the workshop – and perhaps women more generally – lack agency and control over their circumstances.

This idea could also be extended to the males in this story, if 'we' is read as referring to the group of writers: as well as saying nothing to Edward about the harassment, the writers barely stand up for themselves or one another in the face of his criticism that their writing does not represent 'Africa'.

Akunna: She is sent to America because her 'uncle' entered her in the visa lottery, not because she wanted to go. Once in America, her 'uncle' tries to take advantage of her, suggesting that without his help (in return for sexual favours) she could not possibly make her way. Later, she asks her American boyfriend not to buy her presents, but he ignores her and does it anyway – she cannot control even this small aspect of her life.

Ukamaka: While she was with Udenna, she did things his way, to please him; she 'always agreed with him about almost anything' (p.144). The decision to separate was his, not hers. Even when the plane crashes in Nigeria, she can only wait for news: she has no power to contact him or to find out if he is safe.

Chinedu: Though he chose to end his relationship, he did so reluctantly, wishing instead that he had an alternative. As with Ukamaka, his partner had control and did not consider his needs. In addition, his visa has now expired, leading him to lose his job. This forces him to 'feel so uncertain of a future, to lack control about what would happen to him tomorrow' (p.164).

Chinaza: She is forced to be indebted to her aunt and uncle even though their care is minimal and does not take her hopes and desires into consideration. She has no choice in her husband and is completely under his control in terms of living arrangements, food and employment. If she chooses to leave America, she knows she will be at the mercy of her aunt and uncle back in Nigeria.

The protagonist in 'Tomorrow Is Too Far': When she attempts to control her destiny by impairing her brother's success and popularity, she loses control of the situation, and instead her brother dies. Yet she was never able to change her relationship with her mother, and her desires are left unfulfilled; she and Dozie do not end up together.

Examples of agency

In contrast to the examples above, there are a number of instances where characters do demonstrate agency, attempting to dictate to their own lives. Examples include:

- the narrator's small moment of victory in stopping her parents from visiting Nnamabia in prison in 'Cell One'
- Nkem deciding on the family's return to Lagos ('Imitation')
- Ikenna disobeying instructions and returning to the university to retrieve his manuscripts during the attack on Nsukka ('Ghosts')
- Kamara eventually saying yes to Tracy ('On Monday of Last Week')
- Ujunwa/Chioma quitting the bank ('Jumping Monkey Hill')
- Akunna leaving the home and guidance of her 'uncle' ('The Thing Around Your Neck')
- the protagonist of 'The American Embassy' choosing to walk away from her visa interview and remain in Nigeria instead ('The American Embassy')
- Chinaza attempting to leave Ofodile ('The Arrangers of Marriage').

While these and other examples do show characters exhibiting agency, the text argues that these attempts are insufficient, and that in most cases the results will be not worth the effort. It doesn't seem to matter, in a sense, whether they have agency or not; they still have little power over their happiness. For example:

- While Ikenna did survive the attack on Nsukka, he lost friends and his cause, and, looking back on his life, is unsatisfied.
- Kamara does say 'yes' to Tracy but must wait for her to set a day; she has no power to make it happen before Tracy meets the French teacher.
- Akunna manages to find a job and even a boyfriend away from her uncle's, but she barely has money to survive, let alone to educate herself or to visit her family.
- Chinaza only leaves temporarily, and the story is inconclusive about whether she will ever leave permanently.
- Although Ujunwa empowered herself by leaving the bank, her story about Chioma indicates that she knows finding work will be difficult and her options will be limited.

Q Can you identify stories or incidents that demonstrate characters *are* responsible for their fates?

Q If the text argues that events are random, how does it also demonstrate that individuals' decisions can have direct consequences?

DIFFERENT INTERPRETATIONS

Different interpretations arise from different responses to a text. Over time, a text will give rise to a wide range of responses from its readers, who may come from various social or cultural groups and live in very different places and historical periods. Responses by critics and reviewers can be published in newspapers, journals and books, both online and in print. They can also be expressed in discussions among readers in the media, classrooms, book groups and so on.

While there is no single correct reading or interpretation of a text, it is important to understand that an interpretation is more than a personal opinion – it is the justification of a point of view on the text. To present an interpretation of a text based on your point of view, you must use a logical argument and support it with relevant evidence from the text.

Critical viewpoints

Adichie's work, including this collection, has typically been well received by the Western literary community, as evidenced by the numerous literary awards she has received. Although it is more difficult to assess the impact the text has had on African audiences, it has received positive reviews in African media, and Adichie's first novel is part of the Nigerian school curriculum, suggesting that her approach to discussing issues such as the Nigerian Civil War has been welcomed.

Of course, responses to a literary work are always varied. Though many admire *The Thing Around Your Neck*, some critics, such as John Madera in a review for *Open Letters Monthly*, disagree, finding it unfulfilling. Madera argues that Adichie's stories are derivative of the works of 'more accomplished' postcolonial writers, including Achebe – that she attempts similar things but fails to achieve them so successfully. He claims that she writes well technically, but that the stories are 'formulaic' and leave something wanting, and that the collection is ultimately unsatisfying, although he does identify the few elements he feels are effective.

Throughout his discussion, he uses specific evidence or examples from the text to support his arguments. As this review appeared online, reader responses are also accessible in the comments section, and many disagree with his conclusions, demonstrating how different readers will often form different interpretations of a text.

Whether their reviews are positive or negative, critics tend to share a focus on common themes in Adichie's work, including Nigerian identity, the state of affairs for Nigerian women, and the trauma and grief of civil war. Below is a summary of the responses offered by a selection of reviewers.

Aminatta Forna (*The Guardian*)

- Identifies the overarching tone as 'melancholy' and considers the stories to be about 'disappointment and endurance rather than hope'.
- Notes that, like Adichie's novels, this collection is 'suffused with social and political comment', but argues that such content is handled more successfully in her longer works, and that sometimes the determination to cover these areas is detrimental to the text.
- Finds that the stories 'when she concentrates on character, situation or … how lives are changed in a single moment' are the most effective and powerful.

Geoff Wisner (*The Quarterly Conversation*)

- Explicitly argues (unlike Forna) that the short form is just as successful for Adichie as the long, and 'although these stories are not particularly long, there is something important at stake in each one'.
- Identifies the successful use of the second-person perspective, explaining how it draws us closer to the characters and increases the emotional impact.

Susan Salter Reynolds (*Los Angeles Times*)

- Identifies the power of the stories to instil fear in readers.
- Notes the focus on isolated and 'invisible' characters.

- Unlike Wisner, believes that the use of the second-person perspective 'creates a formal distance between writer and readers', rather than increasing intimacy.

Jennifer Makumbi (*African Writers Trust*)

- Like Forna, is focused on the feminism implicit in the stories.
- Also like Forna, identifies a strong sense of melancholy and disappointment in the stories, but associates this with the stories' emphasis on the challenges of being a woman in the Nigerian culture.
- Offers a perspective from within Africa rather than beyond: Makumbi is a Ugandan writer.

Jess Row (*The New York Times*)

- Concentrates on the ways that the collection represents Adichie's experience, identifying in the stories likely reflections of events and details of her life.
- Argues that there is a problematic mismatch between style and content: many of the stories 'collapse under the weight of all that can't be said in the terse, monochromatic sentences of the conventional Anglo-American short story'.
- On the other hand, calls 'Ghosts' 'a nearly perfect story, distilling a lifetime's weariness and wicked humor into a few pages'.

Jane Shilling (*The Telegraph*)

- Identifies family, exile, loneliness and fate as central themes.
- Doesn't explicitly compare the success of Adichie's collection with her longer works, but does note that any 'flaws in the collection' are related to structure; several stories 'simply stop, rather than reaching a conclusion', while the content in 'The Headstrong Historian' seems as though it might have been better suited to a longer form.

Shilling's review, which is quoted on the cover of the Fourth Estate edition of *The Thing Around Your Neck*, suggests specifically that loneliness is actually the 'thing around your neck'. This is a good example of how a reader's bias can contribute to interpretation. (Was loneliness one of the possibilities you identified in answer to the question posed earlier in this guide: what is 'the thing around your neck'?)

Q The above reviews were all published within five years of the book's release. How do you think responses might change in years to come? How might critical responses shift in another ten years? Fifty? One hundred?

Two possible interpretations

As you can see from the variety of responses in the reviews described above, many differing interpretations of a text are possible, as long as they are supported with evidence (examples, specific details and quotations) from the text. Interpretations may be completely valid even when they directly contradict other interpretations, as long as compelling evidence is presented. The possible readings below demonstrate how this might occur.

Reading 1: *The Thing Around Your Neck* shows that no matter how hard Nigerian women try, they can never be in charge of their lives.

Adichie's collection of short stories is full of Nigerian women – both in Africa and in America – who are struggling in circumstances over which they have little control. The tone is often melancholic, and there is scant hope offered that the characters' lives will improve. Many of the central characters in these stories are married, and the collection shows how little power wives have in both minor day-to-day decisions (such as what food to buy, in 'The Arrangers of Marriage'; or how to cook meals, in 'The Shivering') and more significant, long-term decisions (such as where to live, in 'Imitation' or 'The Thing Around Your Neck'). Instead, the males nearly always have the final say, and almost all the husbands in this collection – though not all are cruel or dominating – take charge of their own and their families' lives.

In many stories, we see Nigerian women trying hard to alter their circumstances and take control. For example, in 'The American Embassy' the unnamed protagonist, after losing her son, pursues an American visa from the embassy, undertaking the long waits and beginning the confronting interview. However, despite her efforts, she has no means by which to prove her need for escape from persecution and gives up, remaining in Nigeria. Her husband, in contrast, has already been smuggled out of the country (with her help), and is presumed to be safe in America. Similarly, in the title story Akunna leaves an unsatisfactory situation at the home of her 'uncle'. Yet, on her own she cannot afford an education, and barely scrapes by. These are just two of many examples showing that even when Nigerian women try hard, they still lack the power to take charge of their lives, and instead find themselves at the mercy of the world around them.

The collection is not all bleak, though, and does include several characters who make decisions about their lives, thus empowering themselves; Nkem at the end of 'Imitation' is an example. However, these instances are few and far between, and essentially serve to illustrate how unusual such behaviour is, and how rarely it results in women being able to truly take charge of their lives.

Reading 2: *The Thing Around Your Neck* demonstrates that agency is a direct result of individuals' choices.

While many of the stories in this collection present characters filled with desperation about the situations in which they have found themselves, such characters are contrasted with those who take control over their lives, showing us that when individuals make the right decisions, they can ensure they have agency.

In a number of the stories, characters have begun in difficult circumstances that they have not actively chosen. For example, in 'Imitation', Nkem, while she loves her husband, has ended up living a life (largely without him) in America: a life that she is not sure she wants. Or in 'Jumping Monkey Hill', Ujunwa (as we learn through her fictional persona Chioma) has found herself having to take a job that she does not particularly want or feel comfortable with.

Yet as the stories progress, we see how the characters' decisions change the course of their lives, and give them the agency to shape their own destinies. Nkem decides that she no longer wishes to live halfway across the world while her husband disgraces her by having an affair at home in Nigeria. When he next comes to America, she tells him that the whole family is moving back to Lagos. Although her husband's response is that they will discuss the issue, she knows that 'it is done' (p.42). This demonstrates that her decision has led directly to her empowerment and her ability to shape her life.

Ujunwa, similarly (according to her story), reaches the conclusion that she is not comfortable with the role she is expected to play as a sexualised 'personal contact' (p.110) with the rich clients of the Merchant Trust bank. Although this was the only job she had been able to secure, she has taken a risk and walked away. Not long after her employment with the bank she attends an exclusive writing workshop in Cape Town. Writing had been a passion of hers for many years, and the text demonstrates that through taking action and making a decision, she has given herself the opportunity to pursue a dream.

These and other similar examples serve as inspirations to the other characters who remain trapped in their problematic lives. The text argues that those who do not make decisions to change things will remain powerless. For example, Chinaza very nearly leaves Ofodile, but at the last minute changes her mind, fearful of the repercussions. The text clearly demonstrates the consequences of individuals' decisions, and that individuals can act to change their lives for the better.

QUESTIONS & ANSWERS

This section focuses on your own analytical writing on the text, and gives you strategies for producing high-quality responses in your coursework and exam essays.

Essay writing – an overview

An essay on a literary work is a formal and serious piece of writing that presents your point of view on the text, usually in response to a given topic. Your 'point of view' in an essay is your interpretation of the meaning of the text's language, structure, characters, situations and events, supported by detailed analysis of textual evidence.

Analyse – don't summarise

In your essays it is important to avoid simply summarising what happens in a text.

- A **summary** is a description or paraphrase (retelling in different words) of the characters and events. For example: 'Macbeth has a horrifying vision of a dagger dripping with blood before he goes to murder King Duncan.'
- An **analysis** is an explanation of the real meaning or significance that lies 'beneath' the text's words (and images, for a film). For example: 'Macbeth's vision of a bloody dagger shows how deeply uneasy he is about the violent act he is contemplating – as well as his sense that supernatural forces are impelling him to act.'

A limited amount of summary is sometimes necessary to let your reader know which part of the text you wish to discuss. However, always keep this to a minimum and follow it immediately with your analysis of what this part of the text is really telling us.

Plan your essay

Carefully plan your essay so that you have a clear idea of what you are going to say. The plan ensures that your ideas flow logically, that your argument remains consistent and that you stay on the topic. An essay plan should be a list of **brief dot points** – no more than half a page.

Include your central argument or main contention – a concise statement (usually in a single sentence) of your overall response to the topic. See 'Analysing a sample topic' for guidelines on how to formulate a main contention.

Write three or four dot points for each paragraph indicating the main idea and evidence/examples from the text. Note that in your essay you will need to *expand* on these points and *analyse* the evidence.

Structure your essay

An essay is a complete, self-contained piece of writing. It has a clear beginning (the introduction), middle (several body paragraphs) and end (the last paragraph or conclusion). It must also have a central argument that runs throughout, linking each paragraph to form a coherent whole. See examples of introductions and conclusions in the 'Analysing a sample topic' and 'Sample answer' sections.

The introduction establishes your overall response to the topic. It includes your main contention and outlines the main evidence you will refer to in the course of the essay. Write your introduction *after* you have done a plan and *before* you write the rest of the essay.

The body paragraphs argue your case – they present evidence from the text and explain how this evidence supports your argument. Each body paragraph needs:

- a strong **topic sentence** (usually the first sentence) that states the main point being made in the paragraph
- **evidence** from the text, including some brief quotations
- **analysis** of the textual evidence, explaining its significance, and **explanation** of how it supports your argument
- **links back to the topic** in one or more statements, usually towards the end of the paragraph.

Connect the body paragraphs so that your discussion flows smoothly. Use some linking words and phrases such as 'similarly' and 'on the other hand', though don't start every paragraph like this. Another strategy is to use a significant word from the last sentence of one paragraph in the first sentence of the next.

Use key terms from the topic – or synonyms for them – throughout, so the relevance of your discussion to the topic is always clear.

The conclusion ties everything together and finishes the essay. It includes strong statements that emphasise your central argument and provide a clear response to the topic.

Avoid simply restating the points made earlier in the essay – this will end on a very flat note and imply that you have run out of ideas and vocabulary. The conclusion is meant to be a logical extension of what you have written, not just a repetition or summary of it. Writing an effective conclusion can be a challenge. Try using these tips:

- Start by linking back to the final sentence of the second-last paragraph – this helps your writing to 'flow', rather than leaping back to your main contention straight away.
- Use synonyms and expressions with equivalent meanings to vary your vocabulary. This allows you to reinforce your line of argument without being repetitive.
- When planning your essay, think of one or two broad statements or observations about the text's wider meaning. These should be related to the topic and your overall argument. Keep them for the conclusion, since they will give you something 'new' to say but still follow logically from your discussion. The introduction will be focused on the topic, but the conclusion can present a wider view of the text.

Essay topics

1 'The characters in Adichie's stories lack control over their lives; because of this, they are neither heroes nor villains.' Discuss.

2 How does Adichie's collection explore the notion of identity?

3 'The text argues that people are connected by their similarities and divided by their differences.' Discuss.

4 'The characters in *The Thing Around Your Neck* share a sense of loss and mourning.' Discuss.

5 "If you want to get anywhere you have to be as mainstream as possible." Does the collection support this claim?

6 'Adichie uses narrative perspective to shape the reader's response to the stories.' Discuss.

7 'Because most of the central characters in these stories are women, we have no opportunity to see the males' perspectives.' Do you agree?

8 Akunna "did not know … that people could dictate to life". Can the characters in *The Thing Around Your Neck* 'dictate to life'?

9 'The text demonstrates that difference leads to conflict.' Discuss.

10 'The narratives in *The Thing Around Your Neck* are limited, which is why they are suited to the short-story form.' Do you agree?

Vocabulary for writing on *The Thing Around Your Neck*

Diaspora: People of shared geographical, ethnic, religious or cultural background who have dispersed or moved to places all over the world. The term is often used within postcolonial discourse to describe one of the impacts of colonisation. It can have many different connotations – including the notion of involuntary (or forced) transportation – and refers not just to physical relocation but also to experiences of exile and disconnection from one's origins. In addition, it implies a common experience, and sometimes reconnections with other members of a diaspora, in a new environment. In *The Thing Around Your Neck*, the American stories portray many experiences of Nigerians who are part of a Nigerian diaspora in the United States.

Postcolonial literature: Postcolonialism is a complex academic approach to various fields of study, including literary studies. At its simplest, 'postcolonial' describes something produced in the period following British or European colonisation. Adichie's work is postcolonial.

Protagonist: The central character in a narrative.

Second-person perspective: A narrative perspective using 'you' rather than 'he/she' or 'I'. It can draw readers closer to the subjects of the stories and encourage them to identify with characters. It is rarely used in fiction.

Analysing a sample topic

'The characters in Adichie's stories lack control over their lives; because of this, they are neither heroes nor villains.' Discuss.

The topic presents a general statement (or prompt) about the characters in *The Thing Around Your Neck*. This statement has two parts: an assertion that the characters 'lack control over their lives' and then an assertion that 'because' they lack control they are 'neither heroes nor villains'. You must address both parts of the prompt in your response.

The topic also contains an implicit assumption about values, suggesting that when we view people's lives as being determined by external forces, we do not judge their decisions and behaviours (by calling them 'heroes' or 'villains'). You need to think about this assumption, and consider whether you agree with it, as well as relating it to the text.

You might start by jotting down your initial thoughts about the prompt (including definitions). For example:

- Hero/villain – black and white labels used to evaluate others' decisions, choices and behaviour.
- Having control over one's life means making decisions, choices and changes – not having these imposed by something or someone else.

Consider these questions in relation to the text:

- Do the characters lack control over their lives? If so, to what extent – completely? Or only partly?
- Do some characters have more control (or power) than others?
- Can any characters be considered as acting heroically or villainously?

You can then summarise and connect these ideas in your main contention, as shown, for example, in the final sentence of the sample introduction below.

Sample introduction

Heroes and villains are defined by their behaviour and actions, to which we attribute moral or social value. While there is much suffering and cruelty – and corresponding determination and courage – in *The Thing Around Your Neck*, the characters are not always in a position to make decisions about their actions. Instead, they are often at the mercy of their environments and circumstances. Because they lack control over the key decisions that shape their lives, we are unable to judge their behaviour in order to classify them as heroes or villains.

Body paragraph outline

Paragraph 1: Identify examples of heroes and villains from popular culture or literature to illustrate your definitions of the labels (but keep this brief, as you should focus on the text itself).

- A hero is a person whose deliberate actions overcome danger or hardship and inspire others or improve lives (for example, Australian politician Neville Bonner, cardiac surgeon Dr Victor Chang, schoolgirl peace campaigner Malala Yousafzai).
- A villain is someone whose beliefs, decisions and actions knowingly cause the suffering of others (for example, corrupt public officials, murderer Jack the Ripper, despot Adolf Hitler).
- Literary examples include classic fairytale characters (for example, the wolf and the woodcutter, who respectively endanger and liberate Red Riding Hood).

Paragraph 2: Present examples of characters in the text, explaining how they differ from conventional heroes and villains.

- Nnamabia both commits crimes and acts compassionately and selflessly to help others – he does not fit either label. He is also shown to lack control over events that significantly impact on his life, as neither his imprisonment nor his release are clearly attributed to his own actions or decisions.

- The unnamed protagonist in 'Tomorrow Is Too Far' causes the death of her brother, but the event was outside her control and the outcome unintended; she is not a clear 'villain' because she lacked control over what happened to Nonso.
- While the Hausa woman in 'A Private Experience' takes a risk by helping Chika to safety, the text does not show that this act was premeditated in any way; she simply acted on the spur of the moment in the riot (during which she was unable to ensure her own family's safety), and therefore is not a 'hero'.

Paragraph 3: Discuss how the text portrays characters who lack control over their lives, and how this precludes us from making value judgements about their behaviour.

- Many of the characters have situations imposed on them and are merely responding within these boundaries.
- Even when characters attempt to control their lives, they still lack the capacity to impact on others (for example, Ujunwa left the bank, but still feels powerless to speak up against Edward).
- The pervasive sense of sadness in these stories suggests that the characters cannot change either their own or others' circumstances; if they could, they might be considered heroes or villains.

Sample conclusion

> In Adichie's stories, the characters' lives are often shaped and constrained by external events and circumstances, which in turn can be random and uncontrollable. The lack of control many characters experience means that they cannot easily be seen as simply heroes or villains. They may commit acts that either improve or damage others' lives, but often these acts are unplanned or unintended. *The Thing Around Your Neck* illustrates the complexities and the shades of grey present in all individuals, suggesting that judgements implied by such labels as hero or villain should not be applied to characters unable to control their own destinies.

SAMPLE ANSWER

How does Adichie's collection explore the notion of identity?

In *The Thing Around Your Neck*, Chimamanda Ngozi Adichie explores shared (national) and personal (individual) identities, examining both characters' perceptions of themselves and the ways in which they evaluate others' identities. The collection uses various narrative techniques, including point of view, structure and choice of language, to demonstrate that identity is complex and multifaceted, and argues that identity is central to individuals' existence. In some stories, identity is constructed or revealed through contrast with one's environment, while at other times the collection seeks to demonstrate that though individuals are unique in many ways, people do also share many aspects of identity in common with one another.

There are two main kinds of identity represented in the collection: national and individual identity. While separate, they also influence each other; particularly, as many of the stories demonstrate, one's sense of national character strongly shapes one's personal identity. For example, in 'Jumping Monkey Hill', the writers tease each other about the characteristics common to each of their nations. These perceptions of national identity contribute to Ujunwa's judgement of the people around her – for example, she thinks the black South African has the 'kind of attitude' typical of his ethnic people, and she assesses his identity using assumptions of this kind.

Identity can describe either the way in which one is seen by others or one's internal self-perception, and *The Thing Around Your Neck* explores both. Narrative point of view can dictate which form of identity the reader is led to think about. In the stories written from the first-person perspective, we have insights into characters' perceptions of themselves – for example, James Nwoye in 'Ghosts' considers himself a 'Western-educated man' who is expected to 'laugh indulgently' at his fellow Nigerians who lack such experience. Alternatively, in stories with a third-person perspective, we see how characters classify others – for example, in 'A Private Experience' Chika quickly establishes the other woman's racial and ethnic identity based on her appearance.

In this collection, ethnic identity is one of many variables shown to contribute to an individual's identity and is usually defined with relation to one's environmental or interpersonal context. For example, in the stories set in America, the characters' Nigerian identity is a central theme. This identity is often established by how it differs from that of the characters around them – such as when Chinaza cooks coconut rice and her American neighbour is envious of the traditional recipe. (Conversely, in 'The Shivering' the Nigerian immigrants connect with one another due to their common ethnic identity.) In the African stories, however, characters already share a Nigerian context, so the identities explored are more individual. For example, 'Cell One' offers us the protagonist's perception of her brother's identity; he is 'popular', 'worldly', compassionate and 'charming'. Based on her understanding of who he is, she makes judgements about his likely cult involvement, and about his behaviour throughout the story.

As well as exploring individual identities, the collection explores broader factors contributing to identity, such as religion or marital status. Both are themes that recur in nearly all the stories in *The Thing Around Your Neck*, and the structure (a collection of stories rather than a single narrative) allows Adichie to present multiple explorations of each aspect of identity. In this way, she demonstrates that while there are many common factors contributing to one's identity, the individual result is often unique. For example, wives and mothers are recurring figures in the collection, and share many characteristics – such as being dependent on their husbands and being primary carers for their children – but each also has a separate identity.

Another technical feature of the text that helps Adichie explore the notion of identity is the choice of language, specifically the inclusion of Igbo words and phrases throughout. While most characters speak English, many also use Igbo words. One defining aspect of identity is the language one speaks (representing one's ethnic and cultural background), and speaking two languages is indicative of identifying with two cultures. For example, James and Nnamabia both use English in specific instances, but Igbo at other times (when talking of crime or death). Including the Igbo words in the collection allows Adichie to explore postcolonial and immigrant identities.

Postcolonial, immigrant, ethnic and personal identities are all central to Adichie's collection, and help to situate the stories, provide conflict and resolution for characters, explain events and relationships, and link the themes and ideas that recur in the various characters' lives. Through textual features such as varying the narrative perspective between different stories, Adichie presents a wide range of characters and situations. This allows *The Thing Around Your Neck* to explore some of the many aspects of shared and individual identity, and to examine the contributions identity makes to people's lives.

REFERENCES & READING

Text

Adichie, Chimamanda Ngozi 2009, *The Thing Around Your Neck*, Fourth Estate, London.

Websites

By Adichie

Adichie, Chimamanda Ngozi 2000, 'The Writing Life', *Washington Post*, 17 June, http://www.washingtonpost.com/wp-dyn/content/article/2007/06/14/AR2007061401730.html

——2006, 'Our "Africa" Lenses', *The Washington Post*, 13 November, http://www.washingtonpost.com/wp-dyn/content/article/2006/11/12/AR2006111200943.html

——2012, 'Chinua Achebe at 82: "We Remember Differently"', *Premium Times*, 23 November, http://premiumtimesng.com/arts-entertainment/108378-chinua-achebe-at-82-we-remember-differently-by-chimamanda-ngozi-adichie.html

An article about Adichie's respect for Achebe's work, and about her own interpretations of Nigerian history and particularly the fate of the postwar Igbo community.

——2012, 'Connecting Cultures: Commonwealth Lecture 2012', http://www.commonwealthwriters.org/chimamanda-ngozi-adichie-commonwealth-lecture-2012/

Footage of a lecture given by Adichie, including discussions about her work, its context and production. An engaging insight into the author.

—— 2013, 'Facts are Stranger Than Fiction', *The Guardian*, 20 April, http://www.theguardian.com/books/2013/apr/19/chimamanda-ngozi-adichie-stranger-fiction

Language resources

Widjaja, Michael 2010, 'Igbo–English Dictionary', *Insight into Igbo Culture, Igbo Language and Enugu*, http://www.igboguide.org/vocabulary.pdf

XLingua, http://igbo.xlingua.net/ig

About Adichie

Adichie, Chimamanda Ngozi 2013, http://chimamanda.com

Adichie's official web page. Information is limited, and the page directs readers to Daria Tunca's Adichie website for further detail.

Mesure, Susie 2013, 'Chimamanda Adichie: Dark-skinned girls are never the babes', *The Independent*, 14 April, http://www.independent.co.uk/news/people/profiles/chimamanda-adichie-darkskinned-girls-are-never-the-babes-8572145.html

Nawotka, Edward 2010, 'Interview with Chimamanda Ngozi Adichie, author of *The Thing Around Your Neck*', *The Statesman*, 9 October, http://www.statesman.com/news/entertainment/books-literature/interview-with-chimamanda-ngozi-adichie-author-o-1/nRyZS/

Tunca, Daria 2013, 'The Chimamanda Ngozie Adichie Website', http://www.l3.ulg.ac.be/adichie/

Not Adichie's official website, but a very comprehensive site including biographical information, links, interviews and more.

Reviews

Forna, Aminatta 2009, 'Endurance Tests', *The Guardian*, 16 May, www.theguardian.com/books/2009/may/16/chimamanda-ngozi-adichie-thing-around-your-neck

Madera, John 2010, 'Delightful Gumbo or Strange Brew?', 1 June, *Open Letters Monthly*, www.openlettersmonthly.com/book-review-neck-chimamanda-ngozi-adichie

Makumbi, Jennifer 2013, 'Adichie's *The Thing Around Your Neck*', *African Writers Trust*, 29 January, http://www.africanwritersrust.org/adichies-the-thing-around-your-neck

Row, Jess 2009, 'African/American', *The New York Times*, 27 August, http://www.nytimes.com/2009/08/30/books/review/Row-t.html?_r=1&

Salter Reynolds, Susan 2009, '*The Thing Around Your Neck* by Chimamanda Ngozi Adichie', *Los Angeles Times*, 30 August, http://www.latimes.com/entertainment/news/arts/la-ca-chimamanda-ngozi-adichie3-2009aug30,0,5322197.story#axzz2mw6rSCq9

Shilling, Jane 2009, '*The Thing Around Your Neck* by Chimamanda Ngozi Adichie: Review', *The Telegraph*, 2 April, http://www.telegraph.co.uk/culture/books/bookreviews/5094748/The-Thing-Around-Your-Neck-by-Chimamanda-Ngozi-Adichie-Review.html

Wisner, Geoff, '*The Thing Around Your Neck* by Chimamanda Ngozi Adichie', *The Quarterly Conversation*, http://quarterlyconversation.com/the-thing-around-your-neck-by-chimamanda-ngozi-adichie-review

About Nigeria

Central Intelligence Agency, 'Nigeria', The World Factbook, https://www.cia.gov/library/publications/the-world-factbook/geos/ni.html

Federal Republic of Nigeria, http://www.nigeria.gov.ng

Wikipedia 2013, 'Nigeria', http://en.wikipedia.org/wiki/Nigeria

Other references

Gandhi, Leela 1998, *Postcolonial Theory: A Critical Introduction*, Columbia University Press, New York.